Dear Jennifer

Thanks (
tonight
pushing you
beautiful love
in our world
Ebba

TRUE STARLIGHT

Advance praise

"Ebba's book *True Starlight* is a much-needed contribution to the global conversation that is well under way. She is a survivor, sister, supporter and champion for women and men that are trying to find their true voice, reclaim their dignity and find peace with past trauma. In 2011, I wrote my own memoir (published by Harper Collins). I know first hand it takes strength to step forward and is not always a popular or supported choice. I hope that today we can receive Ebba's story and applaud her for her courage in sharing her journey. Ebba is a wise voice that is truly relatable to many of us. She is an inspirational storyteller and I am grateful to not only support her on her path but stand with her in solidarity."

—**Carre Otis**, American model and actress

"Ebba P. Karlsson is a genuine radiant woman in her own right. In *True Starlight,* she documents her journey with ease and clarity with what can only be said as true spiritual reflection. Once I began her book I thirsted for more. She navigates a part of the feminine journey we can all recognize, but maybe, rarely taken. She is a gifted and talented spiritual woman and I'm glad to see her put her work out in book form."

—**Anaiya Sophia**, author of *Sacred Relationships,*
Sacred Sexual Union & *Womb Wisdom*

"If you have any interest in Consciousness, Christ Consciousness, Oneness, crystals, power spots, ancient sacred places, magic, reincarnation, UFOs, numerology, intentional community, team building, the arts, creativity, self development, self-esteem, psychology, energy, sacred sexuality, marriage, relationships, parenting, travel, pro sports, or dance then there is something in this book for you.

This timely book also addresses the heart of power and sexual harassment in the glamour industries, feminine empowerment, and critical thinking in the face of media mind control. A spiritual journey the likes of which has not been written of since *The Celestine Prophecy*, this book is a gripping story, and a true one. You will find helpful exercises at the end of each chapter drawn from real life experience.

Ebba's brave spiritual journey of healing and self-discovery in this book will empower you to find your own path, to listen to your own inner voice, and to become your true self. I believe you will be able to live in a higher frequency and in a higher vibration after reading this book. If you are seeking healing, happiness and freedom, I invite you to pick up this book. You will almost certainly create more harmony within and around you."

–**Johanna Garrick**, author *28 Days Raw* (28daysRaw.com)

TRUE
STARLIGHT

From Living in the
Shadows to Being Stellar

EBBA P. KARLSSON

NEW YORK

LONDON • NASHVILLE • MELBOURNE • VANCOUVER

TRUE STARLIGHT
From Living in the Shadows to Being Stellar

Published in New York, New York, by Morgan James Publishing in partnership with Difference Press. Morgan James is a trademark of Morgan James, LLC. www.MorganJamesPublishing.com

The Morgan James Speakers Group can bring authors to your live event. For more information or to book an event visit The Morgan James Speakers Group at www.TheMorganJamesSpeakersGroup.com.

ISBN 978-1-64279-030-6 paperback
ISBN 978-1-64279-031-3 eBook
Library of Congress Control Number: 2018937901

Cover Design by:
Rachel Lopez
www.r2cdesign.com

Interior Design by:
Bonnie Bushman
The Whole Caboodle Graphic Design

In an effort to support local communities, raise awareness and funds, Morgan James Publishing donates a percentage of all book sales for the life of each book to Habitat for Humanity Peninsula and Greater Williamsburg.

Get involved today! Visit
www.MorganJamesBuilds.com

DEDICATION

This book is dedicated to you the reader who is looking for something; truth, love, happiness, the perfect partner, the ideal job and who might be hiding behind something. Whether it is your partner's celebrity shadow, or your parent's conditioning, or some organizations, your own fear, or any other beliefs covering the truth—there are many shadows to hide oneself if one chooses to, and the greater the shadow, the greater space to hide.

This book is also dedicated to my beloved husband, Robert, my life partner, and best friend, without whom I would never have made it to where I am today and discovered that I was never in his shadow or any other shadow but that I was only using these as an excuse to hide my own light from the world.

Lastly, I dedicate this book to the younger version of myself since this is the book I wanted to read as a young seeker. When I was younger, most of the feel-good, spiritual, motivational, and inspirational books were fictions or nonfictions where the author would share their modalities, techniques and wisdom to help shift the reader. I needed a real story from somebody who had experienced life and learned the lessons the hard way, and who was willing to be raw and authentic. As a teenager, a young woman, girlfriend, wife and mother, I needed the loving support and comfort that I lacked from the outside world, a guide about how to find myself, to be in relationships and most of all a map to help me navigate.

This book is my life story, but it could be any woman's story. You can see this as a journey through time, through your body, soul, and mind, your chakras. It's meant to take you through your own life, reflecting on your journey, your experiences so that you can be inspired to find your answers within.

This is my journey and where I found my purpose and mission.

Enjoy!

TABLE OF CONTENTS

FOREWORD

When Ebba P. Karlsson asked me to write the foreword to her book I felt honored but also initially confused as to why she chose me out of all people. Ebba wrote that after watching my film "Secrets in Plain Sight" she felt compelled to ask me. She explained that my film, which is my personal exploration of patterns in art, architecture and the cosmos, helped her understand her own journey and the whole reason why she chose to write a book in the first place.

I treasure Ebba's recounting of her soul's journey and admire her courage in sharing her intimate inner world with the impersonal outer world. Although the specific details are always unique, the signposts on all journeys of self-discovery are essentially the same. If you are a seeker, trying to understand who you are and how to live in harmony with yourself and the world, then you have found a book that may resonate strongly and inspire you in your own journey.

Ebba's testimony of repeated sexual abuse at a model agency in Paris bravely exposes not only her personal shadow but points at systemic abuses in the modeling business and culture in general. Her story is very timely and helps us to perceive our collective sexual imbalance, which is thankfully in the process of coming to light.

I feel that Ebba's experience in a Cathar initiation cave in the South of France is a microcosm of what we need to experience in the macrocosm of culture to truly heal the planet and ourselves. In complete darkness she accessed her inner healer (aka higher self) through which she perceived an imbalance in the feminine and masculine archetypes within. This perception, the act of truly seeing, made her an integrated, balanced and transformed person.

By letting go of all the old stories, the baggage and all the negativity she succeeded in her passion project, which in Ebba's case was to become the best ballroom dancer that she could be. Fantastic!

Along her journey she discovered her multidimensional self, enjoyed higher states of consciousness, stumbled upon a portal to higher dimensions at Rennes le Chateau, cultivated awareness of subtle energy, appreciated the power of crystals, experienced massive synchronicity, understood the foundational qualities of number, sacred geometry and so much more.

I've experienced many of the same signposts on my journey and by the universal principle that like attracts like, I appreciate why Ebba chose me to write this foreword. I am grateful for the opportunity to extol Ebba P. Karlsson's timeless wisdom in "You are the one that can set yourself free."

Scott Onstott

http://sacredgeometry.academy

http://www.secretsinplainsight.com

Author's note

Throughout this book, I am sharing my own experience as I remembered the incidents to have happened, they might not be completely correct since some of the things happened a long time ago and my memory might be failing me. I have done my best to share what I have experienced in the way so it should not hurt anyone but also in a way, that I don't compromise with what my feelings at the time were and what my perception of the truth is. To protect the privacy of some of the characters in the book I have changed their names but I have not disguised the names of my family, and I am profoundly grateful to them for their trust in me, and their courage to share the truth.

Don't let the expectations and opinions of other people affect your decisions. It's your life, not theirs. Do what matters most to you; do what makes you feel alive and happy. Don't let the expectations and ideas of others limit who you are. If you let others tell you who you are, you are living their reality—not yours. There is more to life than pleasing people. There is much more to life than following others' prescribed path. There is so much more to life than what you experience right now. You need to decide who you are for yourself. Become a whole being. Adventure.

—Roy T. Bennett

INTRODUCTION

It's the 28th of June, the year is 2017, I'm sitting in our hotel room, number 3301 in Trianon Palace, Versailles, Paris, France. The balcony doors are open, and the fresh country air from the park close to the Chateau de Versailles is caressing my skin as I am writing this.

I see goats skipping around on the fields and two pigeons kissing each other and grooming themselves up on the high oak tree limb outside the window.

I'm getting dizzy again, like I'm entering a vortex, a wind of chaotic energy. Was I feeling the energies from entering the portal and remembering the union of the sacred feminine and masculine that I just had experienced on my sacred pilgrimage? Or was I just extremely exhausted from the last months of stress and hard work?

Goats, pigeons, memories....

What just happened? Where am I supposed to go? Where do I really belong? The questions were many and everything happened so quickly, and this was really the first day I could relax and do nothing in a long while.

A wise person, I think it was Bashar, the wise entity channeled by Darryll Anka, said that in 2016-2017 everything was going to change. But hasn't it always changed? Yes, it has, but maybe not in this way, on this massive scale. Hundreds and hundreds of people are waking up to who they truly are and to their purpose and mission.

I have always been a seeker—a seeker of the truth of happiness, of pleasure, and lots of other things. It took me many years to realize what I know today, and it has been a long journey to discover who I really am, and I'm still discovering it. I think I will never stop, actually, since this is a journey and it will never be about the goal. The journey is the goal and I can honestly say that I have searched many places only to find that what I was seeking for was inside of me all along. I don't know about you, but I have been on a long quest for quite some time. One of my intentions is to inspire you to go on your quest to find who you truly are and what your goals in life are.

The motivation to write this book came from an extremely challenging time. It was as if I had to go through this to get the story out: I experienced a feeling of being closer to a divorce than I ever had been before, was facing a hard and difficult move and one renovation to be exact. (Actually, two moves), Also, I was immersed in more than a full year of studies, starting up my coaching business, struggling with financial challenges, and running a household with two kids and four pets. Maybe I needed all of that to break through my own resistance. Getting the story out has been a very painful process, in that I had to revisit memories from the past that I thought I had let go of, but in remembering I once more had to relive the pain. My new focus on writing took away a lot of the usual attention I paid to my health. That is the story I will honestly share with you.

If I can find my way through my own story, then you can find your way through yours!

I have been preparing for this moment all my life, and I have been waiting to share this with you, to get my message out. But as hardheaded as one can be, it took a lot of removing of resistance to finally jump on this train and do it. I know I have important things to share—things you are going to want to hear. That might sound weird. You might wonder, how the heck can she say that? How can she know that? I know it because we are all connected and I trust that if you picked up this book then there is something in it that you need to know; that you have been seeking for. I will go into that later in the book, fear not. I'm not a crystal ball reader or a psychic, even though my talents in those areas have improved greatly over the years. What I'm talking about here is our natural state of being, and I will explain this further into the book as well. You are reading this book for a reason, and it has been waiting for you.

You might be thinking, How does what I'm reading right now have anything to do with the subtitle of this book: From Living in the Shadows to Being Stellar? I'm telling you that it has everything to do with it because for a long time I stood in the shadows hiding.

This is maybe not the "normal" story about a woman's empowerment after living in the shadows of her husband but a story about finding the true self, the true origin of a being and about a woman that found true empowerment.

Let me take you back about 40 years into the past. I was in fourth grade; it was 1980 in Lidingö, a suburb of Stockholm, Sweden, where I grew up. I was in language arts class. I enjoyed reading as a kid but not to the degree that I enjoyed writing. My little essays would always be about something dreamy and unattainable, like having a horse or being a detective solving a mystery. I lied once in class, and said that I owned a horse, just to make a story better. It seemed to me that the teacher enjoyed reading my essays, even though they were full of fantasy, and I wasn't very good at grammar. To me, the writing was a great escape from the misery I felt in my childhood, and it gave me a sense of peace, and of escaping the chaotic world around me. I guess it might be similar to how people feel when they are playing a video game. I loved to write, and it was one of the ways that I could express to the world what I truly felt.

So, one day after class my teacher came to me and handed back my notebook. She looked me in the eyes and said, "This was really good, Ebba! Maybe you will become a writer one day?" At that time, it seemed so far away that I should become a writer and have anything significant to write about, that it all sounded like a fairytale. Little did I know that there was a seed planted in me that soon would begin to grow. I intend that this book will sow some seeds within you.

So here I am today almost 40 years later, writing my first real book. I am now happily married to my husband Robert, but it takes continuous work to remain happy and I will get into how to do that that more later on in the book. We have two great kids, Thea and Ceasar. We live in Charlotte, North Carolina, USA, together with our three cats: Simba, Sophie, and Grace (that were found in the garden as kittens) and our sweet lady poodle Marta. I want to share my story with you, the story of how I succeeded in getting out of my celebrity husband's shadow and what I did to step into the light, The True Starlight. I want to share it so that you might be inspired by it and start your own quest, finding the answers you are looking for.

I intend that for whatever reason you were drawn to read this book, it will ignite something within you, so that you will discover more of who you truly are.

Welcome to my journey, dear reader. It is my pleasure to serve you with this book in the hope that it will encourage you and inspire you to discover from within who you are, what you want to be, and your life's purpose.

Chapter 1

WHO AM I?

My name is Ebba Karlsson formerly Ebba Palmcrantz; I was born in Sweden in the capital Stockholm on a snowy November night in 1969. It was a tough birth for my mom, and I was sucked out, finding myself with a cone-shaped head. I don't remember much of my early childhood and have always been jealous of my brother Eric who always seemed to remember so much, smart as he is. I'm not sure why I don't remember. Maybe it was deleted from my brain somehow, or it was a conscious choice I made growing up. My parents told me that, once, they had to take me to a psychologist because I would wake up at a certain time every night and stand up in my room. I remember having nightmares of a witch, flying on a broomstick, and coming into my window. I have always wondered whether perhaps it was a real witch or an alien, or if it was some kind of trauma that made me imagine the whole thing. But with age, that sort of experience disappeared.

My grandmother on my father's side was very close to me, and when I was born she wanted me to be called Petra, but my mom insisted that my name should be Ebba. Researchers are not sure about the meaning of the name: if it may be a Viking/Norse name, meaning wild boar and courage. (*Courage* from the French: speaking the words from the heart.) Or if it's more from the Germanic root: derived from *Eberhardt*, meaning strong soul. Some also say it's the feminine form of *Ebbe* meaning The Bear God. It was a common name among 17th century Swedish nobility, but when I was born hardly anybody was called Ebba, and it felt like an old lady's name. As I grew up, I had many nicknames, and I wanted to be called Liz since it was much cooler. Nowadays Ebba is in the top 20 most common names in Sweden, and I feel much better about it, especially since it makes me feel much younger. Little did I know how much my name would come to mean to me—and that courage would be my guiding star, and the bear would be a symbol that has had a great impact in my life. I don't think that the name we get is a coincidence at all, but gives us an energetic vibration to learn from. Do you know the meaning of your name and how it has impacted your life?

Chapter 2

WHAT IS THE STORY BEHIND TRUE STARLIGHT?

When it is dark enough, you can see the stars.
—**Ralph Waldo Emerson**

True Starlight is a term that I came up with after understanding what I was here to do; and after the whole journey that I've done that led me to that understanding. But it started a long time ago. Let me explain: I'm sure you have been admiring pop stars, movie stars, or maybe professional athletes at some point in your life, looking up at them, admiring them, thinking that they are like gods. I know I did; I used to sing Abba's Dancing Queen with girlfriends using a skipping rope as a microphone. Growing up with a famous father, in the music business, I saw them all the time. My dad was on television, has had radio shows, was in the magazines, and mingled with a lot of famous musicians and artists in Sweden during the 60s, 70s, and 80s. He is still rocking as a sound engineer and music producer. Going on 80 years strong, he has produced hundreds of recordings where maybe the most famous one was Jazz at The Pawn Shop from 1976, and he now has a radio show called Happy Jazz. In 1978, when I was nine years old, I got to meet some of the band members in ABBA. It was at the Europa Film studios, where my dad worked, and I was thrilled and proud since they were my biggest idols. It made me feel so special and unique that my dad knew them and had worked with some of them. I remember their energy. It was high and uplifting, and they were so polite. I also felt very seen by them.

Even though they left an epic impression on me, I learned the downsides of fame and glory early on.

As a young child, I didn't understand what was going on, I just enjoyed the ride, hanging out with my dad and so often falling asleep on someone's couch, to the sounds of music and the laughter, while he was in the middle of doing some recording. The hard part was mainly that he was gone a lot and I missed him. It was not until much later that I started to experience the downside of "fame" and I came to understand what I know today. I know many of the old school stars were hardworking artists that worked their way up and not like many of the today's artists that are already screened from early on in their life to be successful. I honestly believe there is much more going on behind the scenes regarding who and why certain people become as famous as they do, and why sometimes really talented artists, that have been working and creating amazing music all their life, never get a chance. It's about who you know and how willing you are to suck up to the powers

Many artists are also extremely miserable, and their glamorous façade is fake. What they are really searching for is validation, recognition, self-esteem, and love. And by seeking it from the outside, they are bound to fail since what they are looking for will only temporarily fill their needs of recognition. True power and true starlight has nothing to do with fame but it is something that is developed from the inside. A true artist is someone who channels that true energy from Source—some people call it the Muse—and who has the passion and diligence to practice being in that state over and over.

I don't know how your childhood was, but mine was very dramatic. My dad's late-night habits started to really get to my mom, and later, when she found out that he was unfaithful, she was devastated and developed a drinking problem. My mom already suffered from asthma, allergies, and maybe some depression as well. These made the whole drinking problem a lot worse, so that it was not the ultimate foundation for bringing up children. I'm telling you, the combination of alcohol and medication is not good! It brought out the worst within her and maybe opened her up for dark energies; I will go into that later in the book.

My mom was successful as a young woman and had been working for the record company EMI where she—amongst many things—translated Walt Disney's movie music into Swedish. Once she got a call to go pick up an English rock band from the airport, but since she was so shy she declined. As it turned out, the band was The Beatles. She was a knockout beautiful blond and looked like a mix of Brigitte Bardot and Claudia Schiffer. No wonder my dad fell at her feet. Even though she was beautiful, she was very naïve and insecure, and struggled with my dad having so many admirers himself. He was not bad looking either, resembling a mix of Gregory Peck and Tony Curtis. After they married and had my brother, and me their relationship got really bad. She did her best as a stay-at-home mom: cleaning, cooking, taking care of me and my brother, and most of the time, handling the money. My dad was a master of his trade, but he was not good with managing money and charging people. We struggled economically and to keep up while living in one of the wealthiest areas of Sweden. So mom had to start working and reeducated herself to become a homeopath, astrologer, and card reader. Yeah, that spiritual, psychic vein I was telling you about earlier probably came from her and her grandmother who was a clairvoyant.

My upbringing was incredibly painful at times since all of my mom's misery, depression, and hate was turned on me when my dad wasn't there to aim at. At times I felt incredibly lonely and had no one to turn to. When I was nine years old, I decided to turn off my emotions. This was of course not done consciously, but out of survival mode, in order to be able to stand the pain. I discovered this years later, going through therapy. I became a very shy girl at first, and over the course of my puberty, I turned from being a very open, friendly, courageous, and feisty young girl into a much colder and tougher girl. By the time that I was 14 years old, I was very depressed. I felt very sad inside, and I didn't know how to get out of the pain I was feeling. I always felt like I had to pretend, to put up a smile and fake it. My mom was very nervous that the neighbors would find out. And I never really knew who the person was that I was coming home to. Was she going to be the sweet mom that I knew she really was inside or would she be the evil queen in Snow White?

One dark night in November, I just knew I'd had enough. I stood by the kitchen window, looking out into the dark garden, and felt like there was simply no reason for me to continue living. I was going to do it. I was so full of revenge and hate, but underneath was lurking a very deep sorrow and pain. My heart felt like it was as black and cold as the winter garden outside. I really wanted to kill myself. In my right hand, I had a sharp kitchen knife, and I pressed it against my skin. I was going to cut myself, to make them all suffer and miss me when I was gone. I pushed the sharp knife-edge harder, and as I did that, I slowly turned my head up to the sky since I didn't want to look at my skin while cutting it. The sky was so beautiful. The stars were so bright, clear, and sharp, almost like they were looking down to me saying, *Hey, do you remember us?* In that moment something shifted inside of me. It was like I had hit rock bottom, and suddenly everything changed. I was embraced by the heavens and the immense love coming from it. Instantly, I knew I could not end my life. I thought, *This is not the end.* It was merely the beginning of my life. And I loved life! How could I, who loved life so much, take my own life? From that day on, I never hurt myself again. Instead I became a seeker, a seeker of happiness and of love, and a seeker of something greater than me. That was the beginning of my relationship to the stars and why I, later on, came to name the power within The True Starlight.

Have you ever felt like you didn't want to live? Like life is too hard and there is no purpose? If so, what made you decide to live? What is your motivation? How do you think we can heal from a difficult past?

Part One

SEEKING

Chapter 3

LOVE—A HARD LESSON

Love is patient, love is kind. It does not envy, it does not boast, it is not proud. It is not rude, it is not self-seeking, it is not easily angered, it keeps no record of wrongs. Love does not delight in evil but rejoices with the truth. It always protects, always trusts, always hopes, always preserves.
—1 Corinthians 13:4-7

My quest for love led me down a long and winding road of boyfriends. I was obviously looking for somebody to comfort and rescue me, someone warm like my dad but faithful. I did find one, and it got pretty serious.

So many times in my life I have been judging others for what I was thinking was ridiculous, weird, or bad behavior. And so many times I had to experience life the hard way and learn the same lessons as the person I had been judging. One of the hardest lessons was when I was only 15 years old. I was about to finish 9th grade and looking forward to the summer break. I was finishing nine years of mandatory school before starting *Gymnasiet*. It's equivalent to Junior College in the USA or like a pre college education. One morning, my father came into my bedroom. His face was pale, and he looked concerned. He looked me in the eyes and said; "I had a really strong dream last night. I dreamed that you became pregnant. You have to be very careful, Ebba!" As the young woman I was, I blushed, laughed, and said; "That will never happen! What do you think about me?" He turned around, still looking concerned, but as though he didn't know what to say next.

About a year earlier (8th grade) I had sexual education class, a very embarrassing subject for teenagers, as you might know. We were watching a video of a young girl who became pregnant, and she had to have an abortion. I was sarcastically saying out loud to my friends, "Well, it's her own fault! And there you go; as you sow you will reap!" Little did I know then that I would face my dad questioning me a year later, and little did he know that I had my sexual debut only six months before he came into my room.

A few months after my dad had this dream I missed my period, so I went to see the gynecologist. She called me later at school and said, "I don't know if this is positive or not for you, but your test came out positive." I just could not believe it! I was only 15, pretty much a child myself, and I was pregnant! I answered, quietly, "No, it's not positive." "I am sorry," she said and hung up. It took a while before I could let my parents know, but when I finally took the bull by the horns, I called my dad, who seemed like the most natural person to call, since my mom probably would go crazy if I told her then.

I said, "You had a true dream. You were right. I am pregnant."

Going into the first year in *Gymnasiet* was a tough one; I was gone the first two weeks because of the abortion. The procedure was done late because I took so long to tell my parents and to get the surgery scheduled. I felt horrible. I got postpartum emotions, and I had breast milk coming out of my breasts. When I told my mom, she became furious; she wanted me to get married to my boyfriend. All of her unprocessed pain came out, and she directed it to me. I was now a prostitute in her opinion. All of my fears came true.

My dad followed me to the hospital as well as my boyfriend; it was a horrible experience as I was fully awake and seeing everything since I only had a local anesthesia. Afterwards, I was put in a room next to a woman 10-15 years older than me who was devastated because she had a miscarriage. *Great! Just make me feel even more guilty and shameful,* I thought. Looking back, I wished that sexuality was something that could have been expressed more easily and that it wouldn't have been so taboo.

Even though I love my mom, she could be so intimidating, especially when she had a drink or two. All of that built up rage within would come out as if she turned from Mrs. Jekyll to Mrs. Hyde. Many times she would act like she was possessed and demonic.

She would chase me around, blame me for my father's unfaithfulness, and call me a slut and evil. Sometimes she would even hit me. Many times she locked my father out, and once she even cut up the clothes in his closet, threw his stuff out of the window, and often called up his friends, and would tell them to get lost or worse. At times I even had to apologize on her behalf to his friends and colleagues. I had no idea of what she was actually going through and the pain she felt inside of her. Years later, when I was an adult, she shared everything with me. I was shocked by her story and that for so long she had been trying to keep the truth from me and my brother. I came to find out that my dad was a sex addict and had cheated on her many times. As I child I would never have understood, I only got to experience her hate and anger and thought it was she who was sick. But today I can honor her for her strength and for trying to protect me and my brother.

My father was my haven even though he was away a lot; he was my idol and my hero. He always had a big, caring heart ready to help the ones in need. And that "need" to please everybody led to him being scattered and unaccountable, which drove my mom mad. I was of course sad when he would leave the house and leave us kids behind every time my mom was drunk and had a horrible outburst. Not even when my dad told me, when I was 10 years old, that he had met another woman, and didn't know what to do, was I mad at him. I just felt sorry for him. It was probably the best I didn't know the facts since knowing the truth would have been very hard and difficult for a child to comprehend.

It must be hard to be a teenager nowadays, since sex and pornography are so easily attainable and not like in my days as a teenager, when sex was a lot more hidden and also, in a way, more innocent. I wished that we had learned how to honor each other and our bodies in school. Even though I grew up in Sweden and nudity was something very natural, we had one bathroom in our house, so seeing my parents naked was the normal thing, sexuality as a sacred art was nothing I was told about. When sex was mentioned in my family especially by my mom, it was filthy, dirty and evil. And it was hidden, taboo. I think society as a whole needs to be re-programmed out of the porn industry. Men and women to heal and to learn about sacred love. Wouldn't it be wonderful if we all got to respect the naked body as the temple it truly is and move away from this sexual programming and distortion that's going on from media and society. I'm sure if we were taught in early age to be natural about our body and our sexuality without all the condemnation and judgment, and learned about true love, all the perversions in society would probably disappear. Look at the native people in contrast to the catholic priest for instance; the more obscure and suppressed sexuality is, the more abominable the behavior. And since I now have a 15-year-old daughter, I talk to her about it, and share with her how important it is to honor one's body. Lately, I found some really interesting facts about energy and sex. Women store men's DNA in their bodies when having sex with them; we also share and mix our energies with each other and create ties that can stay with us for the rest of our lives if we don't clear them or cut them off.

From: www.collective–evolution.com:

The Study

Conducted by immunologists at the Fred Hutchinson Cancer Center in 2004, the study took samples from 120 women who had never had sons. They found that 21% of these women had male DNA. The women were then categorized into four groups, according to pregnancy history: Group A had had only daughters, Group B had had one or more miscarriage(s), Group C had induced abortions, and Group D had never been pregnant before. The prevalence of male microchimerism was considerably greater in Group C, although it was still present in each group: Group A showed 8%, Group B showed 22%, Group C showed 57%, and Group D showed 10%.

From these results, researchers hypothesized possible sources of male microchimerism as known pregnancies, miscarriages, vanished male twins, or sexual intercourse. This means that through intercourse alone there is a potential for women to hold onto male genes and DNA within their organs and bloodstream for their entire life!

Knowing this made me understand better the concept of taking on someone's energy when we have intercourse. We do merge, not only physically, but also energetically and spiritually as well. I wish I had known that, years ago as a young woman trying her wings, since I didn't stop dating boys and being a heartbreaker. If you happened to be one of those of hearts I broke, reading this book, I am genuinely sorry that I broke your heart.

Chapter 4

PEACE—MEDITATION

The secret of health for both mind and body is not to mourn for the past, worry about the future, or anticipate troubles, but to live in the present moment wisely and earnestly.
                                                    —**Buddha**

Even though I grew up in a very chaotic upbringing, there were also a lot of good things. My parents were sensitive, warm hearted and caring at core and they also had a crazy kind of humor. The humor and playfulness was two of the things that really made us all survive the craziness and chaos that we had brought up on ourselves. It was funny how many of me and my brothers' friends who had a tough time, were drawn to our family and often came to our house to hang out. Maybe because of the one thing that kept us sane the most: the deep spiritual interest that my parents shared, and the seeking of truth seemed to be a common thread. My parents went to see Ambres, an entity channeled by a Swedish man called Sture Johansson who later was depicted in the movie with Shirley MacLaine, *Out on a Limb*. Ambres had a considerable impact on my parents, and they both had some strong previous life experiences going to see him. I recall listening to their conversation and always feeling left out; why didn't they ask me what I thought about it? I knew so much about these things, I thought to myself.

As I grew older, the seeking remained. I remember my grandparents on my mother's side who lived as retired pensioners in a quaint village on the coast of Spain when I was growing up; my granddad had a massive library with books and interesting artifacts from all over the world that he had collected on his trips. Many of his books were about the paranormal, spiritual development, ancient civilizations and technologies as well as UFOs and he had a deep interest in those subjects. Since I was a curious child, I liked to poke around in his drawers looking at insects that he had dissected and pinned, as well as his amazing collection of stones and fossils. He did not approve, by the way, but he acknowledged my curiosity and wanted to experiment with me. He took out a big dictionary and put it bluntly on the table, pulled a page up, and said, "Ok so let's try this telepathy experiment. You will close your eyes and try to see what I'm looking at, and then from your inner eye, try to perceive what it is and draw it." I was actually good at drawing, so I enjoyed the little challenge he put up. After a while, he asked me to stop and let him have a look at what I had drawn. He smiled as he looked at my drawing and slowly pushed the book over to my side so that I could see the photo he looked at. To my huge surprise, there was a house there, looking much like in the picture I had drawn.

My mom started to study as soon as my brother and I were big enough to walk to school, and she shared many of my grandfather's interests. She became a passionate astrologer, a card reader, and homeopath. This gave her life more meaning, and we all benefited from her knowledge. My first year in *Gymnasiet* was a disaster since I was gone the first 2 weeks from school due to the abortion and it left me feeling very insecure. I also didn't have a lot of peace at home, which led to my grades being deficient. Even though I always loved to learn, studying under pressure was never my thing. That fall I did have a significant release of this pressure since my dad, mom, my brother, and I started Transcendental Meditation. We went to see this really charming guy called Peter, who lived in a small one-room apartment. We could sense the incense filling up the entry of the apartment block as we entered the building, and coming into his studio was like entering a gateway to India. He was a slim and gentle man with kind eyes. He offered us green tea, and we drank it for the first time in our lives. Afterwards we sat on his only couch and let him instruct us in this delicate art of mindfulness.

Learning to meditate was a gift from the heavens. It gave me so much peace inside, space where I could finally breathe. We connected in a whole new way as a family, and I could finally be more myself and feel a connection to the big all, the one, Source. On top of that, my grades got better, and I performed better in PE (physical education) as well, and I became a happier person. I loved that we could meditate together and the whole idea of creating a better world with that as a base was thrilling. Peter was also part of starting a group building project, an ideal village where everybody would meditate and help each other. It would be called The Ideal Village where the houses would be environmentally friendly and built according to *Vastu Shasta*, the Ayurvedic method of constructing houses, kind of like the Indian version of Feng Shui. My family and I were offered a chance to participate in this group project in Sweden and buy a lot to build on. Of course we couldn't afford it at the time, but we used to dream about buying a lot there and building the perfect house.

I have continued to meditate since then and have tried many different variations to find out which one works best for me. There was a time in my life where I could simply not sit and meditate, and doing active meditations—such as dynamic meditation where one moves to music—was an important part of getting in touch with my inner peace. Today my meditation is only sitting watching my breath for 10-30 min per day and my goal is to do it every day. The days I go without are very different, as I don't feel as focused, relaxed, and connected. There are apparently many ways of meditation, and as there are active and passive meditations, you have to find out which one works best for you. I encourage you to try it out, if you haven't already. There are so many amazing benefits that come out from it. Science has proven that twenty minutes of meditation is the equivalent to four hours of sleep. Some of the benefits are: gaining inner peace, increased self-awareness, becoming more grounded and calmer, lowering blood pressure, and growing inspiration. I simply can't understand why this is not a subject in school. The whole society would benefit from it.

What was your first connection to spirit and source? Was it through religion or tradition? Or was it something you discovered within? Have you ever tried to meditate and how was that for you? What ways do you connect to yourself and to source?

Chapter 5

APPROVAL—MODELING

How people treat you is their karma. How you react is yours.
—Wayne Dyer

I n 1992, I had full-time employment at The English Body and Hair Care Company, The Body Shop, and just before my holiday, I had been approached on the street by a scout and modeling agent. His name was David. He seemed to be trustworthy, as he knew some friends of mine, so he wasn't a total stranger. He said, "Hey Ebba, do you work as a model?" And I had done some smaller commercial jobs so I answered yes, and then he continued, "You should come down to France, and I'll get you some work. You could earn some money you know." I was flattered. We exchanged numbers. I started thinking about it. I really wanted the money, and to have the chance to be a successful model was, of course, something that was very tempting. So I decided to use my holiday to go down to Monaco to meet up and try my wings. I didn't have a cell phone. They were pretty rare then. So we decided to meet at a certain address and, since I had visited Monaco once before on a language school trip in 1987 when I was 17, and had studied French for 6 years in school, I spoke some French. When I arrived in Monte Carlo and got off the bus, he wasn't there. I waited and waited, but he never showed up. I became nervous and called the number he had given me from the phone booth. Luckily, he answered, or maybe I wasn't so lucky. He sounded surprised that I was there, "I didn't think you were coming." "Well, I told you I was," I answered. He finally came down to the *Tabac* where I was waiting. He didn't seem too interested in having me there. We walked back to the place where he was staying. It was one of the tallest buildings in Monaco just by the Parc au Casino. David was staying with an older businessman that ran a fashion business. The businessman told me that he had needed swimsuit models for his fall collection. But it turned out I was too late, and he didn't need any at that time. He was sweet and wanted to help so he said, "Well I do need a secretary, and you speak French? Would you be interested?" I looked at David with a question in my face. Was this the reason he brought me here? David later told me, "No, I will get you another job."

We were invited to stay in the apartment for the night. The following day, we walked around in Monaco and in the evening, David introduced me to a good friend of his, an older lady who was very sweet. She said: "If you ever need anything let me know." In retrospect I wish I had listened to her and kept her number, but I had no clue what I was getting myself into. We stayed another night there, and then he gave up on Monaco and took me to Cannes. David said, "I have a friend there, and we can stay at her house." It turned out the friend was not home, but he told me not to worry: "We can stay in the pool house until she gets back." We went into their garden in back of the house. There wasn't a pool house there, but a small shack. I started to feel very uncomfortable. For some reason, the pool shack had mattresses on the floor. It was like somebody had just been sleeping there, which I thought was very weird. Now I started to get really worried. What was David up to? He wouldn't leave me alone. David started to tell me that he was really attracted to me, and he thought I was beautiful, and his hands were all over my body. He was at least 10-15 years older than me, and I thought he was slimy and disgusting. I want to throw up when I think about what I let him do to my body. As I was telling him no, no, several times, he desperately insisted on having sex with me. I was too frightened to resist. Of course, looking back, I wish I had, but he was a lot stronger and as I was relying on him, I was an easy prey.

One day when I was alone in the pool shack, I looked in his passport; his name was not David and I became terrified. He had lied and abused me and I didn't even know who he was. I needed to get of there quickly, so when he came back, I told him I had to call my parents. We had to walk down to the village and call from a phone booth. But as I called them, he stood outside listening carefully to every word I said. I didn't dare to tell them what was going on as the only thing I knew was that he was not David, and I couldn't trust him. After I hung up with my parents, I panicked, thinking, *What should I do now?* On the walk back, I desperately threw out, "When are you going to fix me the job you promised?" He said, "We are going to Paris. I will get you a job there."

We went to Paris, and to my relief we stayed with a gay guy. His name was Paul and he had a new modeling agency called Champagne. At least now I had a bed of my own and wasn't in the claws of David, the creepy monster agent. The new situation was somewhat better, but when I reached out to pick up something from the floor, to my horror I found a whole stack of gay porn magazines underneath the bed. Yuck!

While David was trying to get me a job, I strolled around the streets of Paris and by coincidence met a guy from Stockholm that I knew.

He was there working in a shop helping a relative. He called me from the storefront, and we started talking. I shared a little bit what had happened to me, and he became furious. As soon as David came back and they started talking, my friend told David to take really good care of me. He should not have done that; David became furious and started to threaten me.

The following day I sat in a café and started talking to the bartender. He was a very friendly American guy, my age. We decided to meet after his work and we went for a walk and had a very nice and friendly conversation. I finally felt I found someone I could trust.

He then invited me to his flat to have a drink and chat, but as soon as we got there he wanted to have sex! After what I had been through it was the last thing on my mind. I was seriously wondering if the word SEX was written on my forehead? I was very disappointed since I needed a friend, not a freaking sex-buddy.

Finally, David got me set up for a casting call at the most famous modeling agency in Paris and maybe even in the world: ELITE. It was owned by Gérard Marie and was representing all the supermodels like Linda Evangelista, Kate Moss, Cindy Crawford, etc. It was a beautiful office on 21 Avenue Montaigne. When I got into the agency, I was very impressed; I didn't know at this time where I was and how famous this place was. The staff members were surveying me from head to toe as I passed them while they were all talking on the phone. I was taken to Mr. Gerard's office, and at that time, I thought his name was Jean-Claude, but I must have mixed all the names up since Claude Haddad was one of his notorious scouts. I have a really hard time remembering everything now when I write it since there is a part of my brain that just wanted to wipe out all the following memories. Inside Gerard's office, I shook his hand, and he invited me to sit down. He started talking immediately about a possible career as a famous model that I could have and as he did that, he turned all the shades down on the windows, which I thought was weird since it was the middle of the day.

He pulled out a large portfolio with some of the top models in the world and pointing at a Swedish woman, he asked me if I knew who she was? And I did. Of course she and all of them were indeed famous. He asked me what I wanted to do with my life and why. And how I was going to earn big money. He started explaining to me all the jobs I could be doing as a model and since I spoke French, he had some interesting movie roles coming up. After maybe what seemed like an hour of brainwashing, he asked me: "What do you think this Swedish model did to become so famous?" And he made sure I understood his message: If you want to be like her and better, having six-figure contracts, you have to give something back. As he said that, I felt his hand up my skirt, and his fingers penetrated my vagina.

I completely froze! What had just happened? I was scared of doing something wrong, so I slowly pulled away and said I had to think about it. When I came out of his office, all the staff glared at me, like they knew what was going on in there day after day.

I left the scene behind me and sat down on the first available bench. I was so shocked. I couldn't understand what had just happened. I felt so confused and so filthy. How could I have been so stupid that I didn't see this coming? My tears started rolling down my cheeks as I felt like the loneliest person on the planet. I just wanted to go home and hopefully wake up from this horrible nightmare. I panicked. I didn't know what to do. And I must have been in shock during the whole day because later the same night I was invited to Gerard's private apartment for a casting, and I decided to go, thinking what happened to me earlier must have been a one of a kind incident. David was there too. It was a relief to not be the only one there that evening. I had kind of expected some comfort but instead to my horror, he had several girls living there, and they were a lot younger than me, the most youthful maybe 17 or younger. And some of them were not in good health either; this was not the place to open up or try to find sympathy. Most likely we were all in the same boat. Gerard mentioned he had just had a famous American movie actor there to pick up a girl for the night to go out with. I was once more shocked and disappointed especially since this was one of my favorite actors and I couldn't believe that he would do such a thing. A lot more girls showed up. Maybe 10. And we had to get undressed and only wear underpants so they could see our breasts. *How insulting*, I thought. But maybe this was how it worked in the industry?

I can't remember who else was there, but it was either Claude or some other guy, looking at us and taking notes. I felt like a cow at an auction being judged from head to toe. Am I a good specimen to breed?

After that experience, I realized this was a nightmare situation and I had to get out of this hellhole before it was too late. I came to realize that my dreams had been shattered and I was so disappointed; this was not the fashion industry I wanted to work in. So I came up with a plan. I lied that I had to go home to Sweden and finish my driver's license and then I would come back and start working for them. I finally got my airplane ticket so I could go back home. Back in Stockholm, I swore to myself to not tell a single soul what had happened. I felt this was totally my fault. I couldn't blame anybody for what had happened even if I wanted to. I was disgusting, and my innocence was ripped off forever. Just because I was so vain and thought I could be a new Cindy Crawford.

It was so hard to grasp that the beautiful ladies I had seen on the covers of the magazines and on the walls at the agency had most likely been through the same or similar experience as me.

My current boyfriend was so happy to see me. I was so happy to see him too, but as soon he came close, wanting to be intimate with me, I pushed him away in disgust. He felt very neglected of course and hurt. I could not tell him. It became worse, and he thought that I had met somebody else. I then realized I had to tell him the truth.

I told him the full story of what had happened. He was so pissed off. He went off to find David who now was back in town and took out all his rage—and some of mine—on him, so according to the rumors, he needed a significant amount of stitches to fix his face. I was proud that my boyfriend stood up for me and I got some revenge but at the same time I didn't even want to know what exactly had happened because I was terrified that David and the whole team from ELITE would come after me.

But nothing happened besides a rumor reaching my boyfriend: that I had gone to bed voluntarily with David. My boyfriend, the poor thing, didn't know what to believe and started doubting my story.

I should have gone to the police, but that thought never crossed my mind until several years later, when I read in the evening newspaper *Expressen* about the big raid that had happened at Elite. I realized that this was a drug and trafficking business. At that time the phrase *sex trafficking* didn't exist as far as I know. Even though there were so many women that came forward claiming that they were being sexually abused by Gerard Marie and his scouts, there was not one conviction. He was a mighty man with a lot of convincing connections that helped him out. BBC did a documentary about him and the drugs and sex abuse, but despite that, the bastard is still on the loose and running another agency.

If you have ever been abused, you know how awful, guilty, and shameful one can feel. Looking back, I still feel disgusted about the whole thing and sad that I didn't have more guts to stand up for myself and run away. It is never ok for anybody to go beyond a person's boundaries. I wished that I had more courage to say no, without being fearful for the consequences a no would have. I know I did my best at that time, but I have come to understand that I was so conditioned and fearful of saying no. If I did it, it would have had negative consequences. It wasn't proper for a girl to say no at all in fact, to stand up for oneself. One should obey. Maybe this wasn't only in my family but as a society as a whole, as a Swede? We don't say no enough in Sweden. It's even considered selfish perhaps, so we say yes to almost everything, even though it might be hurting us as a nation. I have learned how fragile and innocent young women and men can be, especially if they are looking for love and confirmation outside of themselves—many do since they often didn't feel loved as a child—and how easy it is to be fooled by what we think we want. The shame was also that I thought that I had failed: failed in becoming a famous model, failed in being a faithful girlfriend, failed in being a good daughter, and I had failed in listening to my inner voice.

If I had known as a young woman how to fill myself with love internally, and learned how to listen to my higher self within, this whole thing would probably never happened, but it did. I know for myself that the incident happened for a reason and I have learned a lot, grown, and have become a more humble being, and I am better at reading others' intentions. But most importantly I can say no today, something that was very scary before. The challenge is that sometimes I have become overly suspicious. It took a lot of courage to heal since I had to disclose my story and admit my "failure". Then when I understood that it wasn't my fault and I didn't fail, I had to face the anger and hate I felt for the abusers, before I was able to forgive. By doing all these things, I also had a great win since I discovered more of myself. Today I have forgiven the abusers, but I have not forgotten what they did. The scar is still there to remind me of the past. I know these guys were most likely abused themselves once at some point, and I know the Day of Judgment will come: if it's not this lifetime, it will be the next. That's the law of Karma: that they will have to personally experience the effects of everything they have caused.

I know today that I was not the only one being abused, and doing research on my past, I found out about one other woman who had the courage to share her story. Her name is Carré Otis and she wrote the book, *Beauty, Disrupted*. She was a very successful model at ELITE and was raped by Gérard.

Chapter 6

FREEDOM—HOW I MET ROBERT

There are only two days in the year that nothing can be done. One is called yesterday and the other is called tomorrow, so today is the right day to love, do and mostly, live.
—the Dalai Lama

After a few years of managing and thriving at the Body Shop store, making it with my team one of the most successful ones in Sweden, even though this was a great company that gave me a lot of opportunities to grow, I started to get bored and wanted something more interesting in my life. I then met a lady called Kathrine, about my mother's age, who liked my enthusiasm. We shared many similar ideas, and we decided to start to work together building up a new business. It was my dream business:

The Grail, A Holistic Therapy Center, with a restaurant, a shop, classes, and different healing modalities. At that time we didn't have anything like it in Stockholm and I had a longing to create something that could introduce more alternative methods to people and bring forth more healing. I took the name The Grail since it would inspire people to find their chalice of eternal life as that was what I thought it represented at that time.

I was an energizer bunny with no knowledge at all of how to run a big company like that.

And she had the money and some knowledge so off we went.

It was so tough. I had taken on too many things at the same time and was totally overwhelmed, something that happened over and over in my life, like a big action addicted junky, who would go into withdrawal if life stood still just for a moment. My lady friend turned out to not be as knowledgeable as I would have liked, so she couldn't help fix the situation. After six months of hard work, and a150,000.00 Swedish crowns loss, I found myself totally burned out—and since I didn't have any money or a job, I was devastated.

To my rescue came Roger Nilson. He was a charismatic man about 20 years older than me, a fierce sailor and a competitive Whitbread navigator who sailed around the world, challenging himself. He had met his fears facing death on the seas, but as he said himself, the most significant fear he ever had to face was himself. I met him a few months earlier during one of the great team building conferences we had at The Body Shop, where he had shared his epic journey and his understandings about leadership and teambuilding.

I was so mesmerized by his story; I asked him if he could be my mentor for the new project that I was working on. This was during the time I was building up the Grail. And after I got burned out, he recommended that I should go to do this leadership training that had changed his life.

He was talking about this place south of Stockholm by the Sea called Mullingstorp, where many of the exercises were inspired and taken from the Esalen Institute, a retreat Center in California and also from the teachings of the Indian guru OSHO.

After some consideration, I decided to go together with Kathrine, who I was working on the Grail with. On the way there, I had a powerful sensation in my body and stomach. I just knew I was going to meet the man of my life. I thought to myself, *Oh my lord, I'm not ready for that! I'm just the most screwed up girl on the planet.* I still had an on/off relationship with my dancing boyfriend since six years back, the one who hit the disgusting agent in the face. And I was kind of dating another guy who lived in New York.

As we were approaching the center, the feelings got even stronger and when I got out of the car and walked up the pathway, I saw him! And he didn't look at all what I was expecting him to look. He was tall, had blond hair and blue eyes, like a typical Swede. I had always been drawn to dark-brown-eyed guys, more the exotic, Southern European, and mixed kind. He was way too Swedish for me! He wore a black and yellow Ralph Lauren sweatshirt and blue jeans. He was looking down into the gravel while he was scraping the gravel with one foot. He was talking to an older gentleman next to him. I got closer, and he looked at me. I had no clue who he was, but I found out that he was a very good professional golfer, and I didn't know anything about golf! The closest I had come to a golf course was driving a dirt bike on it (to Robert's horror!) when I was 15. To me, golf was a boring game made for boring, old, rich people like my neighbor where I grew up. I had some things to learn.

The workshop was a three-day leadership training for executives, and during that time, Robert and I got to know each other pretty well. Many of the exercises were done in pairs, and we ended up with each other a lot of the time. As the course proceeded, he came closer and closer with each exercise. At the end of the training, I ended up doing a tarot card reading for Robert, and we went for a walk. He made it clear that he thought I was boring since the only thing I was talking about was myself. That came as a shock to me as I thought I was interesting and that he was boring.

Robert turned out to be much more interesting than I had imagined. And his highly magnetic being drew me closer and closer to him. He had something that I simply couldn't resist and that I wanted more of. As I got to know him, I realized he was a complex person and very intelligent. This was a guy, besides being utterly handsome and attractive, I could actually have a decent conversation with, in comparison with a lot of other men that I had met. He challenged me to look at my own beliefs and was very inquisitive, as if we had been coming from two different planets.

The exercises at Mullingstorp made me experience my emotions through my body and not only in my head. The founder of Mullingstorp, Dr. Bengt Stern wrote a book, *To Feel Bad Is a Good Start*. That book made a difference for me, as I stuffed my emotions so deep in my body that it seemed to take forever to be able to be vulnerable and open up.

I had protected my pain from being exposed for so long due to my survival mode growing up in a painful family situation and also from the painful experiences in France. At Mullingstorp, I started the journey of going back to my childhood and reawakening and re-experiencing the pain that I needed to face to become a more free person.

These exercises, based on body psychotherapy, are not always needed to make a difference, but to me, they were an essential part of not being afraid of who I am and of my emotions. Later I decided to do much more training there. My first course was called Meet Yourself, and skilled therapists who helped me to heal my wounds and discover more of my power carefully guided it.

For instance, many of the exercises took me back into childhood where I had to relive the pain to be able to heal and let go. I later came to work as an assistant to deepen my journey.

As I peeled off the layers of pain and conditioning, Robert got to see more of who I was behind the tough mask I had carried so long. And as we spent a lot of time together at Mullingstorp, our relationship started going beyond the traditional dating and we got to know each other on a deeper level; that would be the foundation of our relationship. We saw each other cry, dance, laugh, and explode in anger as we explored ourselves during the exercises. We saw the things within each other that we were missing the most within ourselves; I was lacking that commitment to one thing at a time, while Robert found my wildness liberating and fun. By the time we became a couple, the people working there used to say that when we first met, there were sparkles in the air between us.

Have you ever had a hunch of meeting someone? Have you had an inner knowing? What was it like and can you remember how it felt? Did this person become somebody special in your life? If you have a partner, how did you meet? What was it that was so attractive about this person? Do you think the person had qualities that you needed to develop within yourself?

Part Two

FINDING

Chapter 7

A TASTE OF THE
LAW OF ATTRACTION

Man, alone, has the power to transform his thoughts into physical reality; man, alone, can dream and make his dreams come true.
—Napoleon Hill

Many times in my life, I have experienced The Law of Attraction without even knowing that it existed. Sometimes I have wondered if life is already written in the stars just as my mom has always said, and if the things that would happen in my life have been planned to occur all along. It is like I was given a map to follow at birth: like God saying, *Here, you go my child. Just follow this way, and you will get the necessary experiences that you need.*

One of those experiences happened when I was 19 years old. I had come back from studying Spanish in Spain and was working, helping my dad as a sound engineer. My mom was reading a magazine, and in there was an article about Anita Roddick, the founder of the English hair and body care franchise company: The Body Shop. I remember reading the article and was mesmerized by her and her fantastic business idea. I had a strong feeling and longing to be part of it and said out loud to my mom, "I want to work here!" At that point, I didn't know that the store even existed in Sweden. Several years later, I found myself looking for an extra job, and a friend told me about the new Body Shop store that she worked in. At that time I didn't even remember the article my mom had shown me. I got the job and started working extra at the store in the Old Town of Stockholm; it was the first Body Shop in Sweden. Later, in some mysterious way, I became a manager of one of the other stores in Stockholm in 1992. Interestingly enough, the new store was inaugurated on my birthday, and superstitious as I was, I saw that as a great sign.

I was also very lucky to meet Anita in person a few times, and she was my heroine. I remember being in her beautiful old brick house outside Brighton, England and looking at her family picture. It was one of those huge custom oil paintings that was purposely put on the mantelpiece to radiate union and warmth in the house, as only a great family picture can do. I wrote in her guest book, "Someday I'm going to be like you." Her life reflected everything that I thought I wanted to be; she was smart, intelligent, a courageous businesswoman that had changed the whole beauty industry with her passion. She stood for so many good things that I longed to be and have. I was disappointed when I found out she had family issues like most of us have. But she has always inspired me to pursue my dreams and that nothing would be too hard to change or overcome.

25 years later Robert and I have the same kind of painting of our family hanging above our mantle piece. Simply amazing how the thing we want so strongly but don't cling to can be created in our own lives.

Have you ever experienced something similar where something happened in your life that at first didn't make sense but later it evolved into something completely different? I believe that everything we do has a purpose and is leading us forward and—if we are awake enough and take our chances—it takes us forward to where we need to be.

CHAPTER 8

HOW THE LAW OF
ATTRACTION WORKS

*I attract to my life whatever I give my attention, energy, and focus
to, whether positive or negative.*
—Michael Losier

I t was the summer of 1996. I was working on a vision quest that
I was doing with my family as a kind of a group therapy that
was taught by a lovely Canadian friend of my family, Sandy. She

had a company called On Purpose and was teaching a lot of different techniques based on the Book; *The Course in Miracles*. My mom and I were sitting on the balcony writing down our visions in our notebooks. I was drawing the house that I wanted to live in and stating that by the end of next year, I should have enough money to pay my debt (debt from running my former business, the Grail). I had no idea at all how it was all going to work out, but I really liked the process and thought it was fun. I think that after it all was completed, I completely forgot about it.

About one year later, in the summer of 1997, Dr. Bengt Stern recommended that I go with Robert and work for him, as his assistant. And since I had just been certified as a Personal Trainer I could go on tour with him and help him out with his physical training. Just before that, I had followed him on some of his tournaments, and I really enjoyed it. Our first week together was somewhat tragic. His grandmother had just passed away, and he was sad. We were in Ireland at the Irish Open. My role as his assistant was to help him with a special diet he tested, find a gym where he could work out, spot him, help him stretch, and give him some light reflexology that I had been taught to perform by Dr. Stern. My deal was to get a percentage of Robert's prize money. I thought it was a great deal, and I enjoyed going with him. But Robert didn't play so well the first week. The following week we were going to the BMW Open in Munich, Germany. At the airport, we needed some cash, so Robert asked me if I could go and change some money for us. I did, and when I counted the different currencies (we didn't have Euros then) I saw that one of the Italian liras had something written on it. I read and spoke some Spanish, but Italian was a little too hard to understand, and since I was so curious, I went to ask one of the Italian golfers if he could translate for me. It was Constantino Rocca, a lovely Italian player about ten years older than Robert and me. He read it and told me what was written on the note with a smile.

'The person who receives this note shall have great luck. As long as he is writes this message on another 3 notes and passes them on' Since I was so superstitious, I took on the assignment.

The whole week was nerve-wracking since it was my second tournament and I had no experience whatsoever. Robert played really well, and it hit me that I had only written two notes and hadn't finished writing the third note, so I quickly finished it. By the end of the day, Robert beat Carl Watts in a four-hole playoff. Robert won the tournament and we were so excited. What a great start to my career as Robert's assistant. Soon we were off to the next tournament, The Canon European Masters, which was played in Switzerland, in a small, quaint village in the Alps. In my excitement I had forgotten to give the notes away after I had finished writing on them. When buying a coffee I found the notes and quickly finished my assignment. Crans Sur Sierre was a very posh village where the golf course was at 2000m above sea level and where the rich and famous would go and ski in the winter. Robert continued to play well during the week. After another exciting weekend of golf, Robert finished in second place, and to our great surprise, Constantino Rocca won!. Wow! The Law of Attraction had worked wonders. From then on, every time Constantino met me he always asked, "Do you have another of those notes?"

Unfortunately, I have not seen another one since then. But interestingly enough the hostess of this tournament in the years to come would be the famous super model, Cindy Crawford. I never got to meet her in person, but when Robert won there in 2002 he got a hug from her. A Swedish commentator mixed Cindy and me up while he was commentating the tournament on TV, and mistook her for being me. Realizing his mistake, he said that he thought I was much prettier. I am sure he said that just to be kind to me, since I couldn't be there in person and he wanted me to feel better. That meant a lot since I always thought she was stunning and once wanted to be like her.

With Robert's first and second placements, I was beyond happy! Over the last two weeks, I had made enough money to pay off my debt and also had enough money to treat myself. We were in Crans Sur Sierre, Switzerland, the mecca of watches, where they had many exclusive shops, and one them offered great deals for the players. I took the opportunity, and I bought myself a watch: my first token of commitment, luxury, and celebration. It was a gold and stainless steel Ebel, Discovery model, the unisex style that was as big as my wrist. And I had never bought something that expensive before. I was so proud. I was also so relieved to be able to pay off my debts. Now I could start fresh again.

Lately, I have been reflecting on how it was even possible that this could happen. I do believe in The Law of Attraction, and I work with it with my clients. I have come to the following conclusion: We are living in a world of energy, and some say a hologram, where we are the creators of our own life. We create with our minds, and we can allow this creation to take form in the third dimension that we are living in. I think there is a constant flow of energy, existing all the time. Whether it's positive or negative, it is energy that is available to us, and with our focused intent, we can manifest things we desire into our physical reality... The key then is to allow it to happen: by trusting that what is meant to come will come in the best timing.

> Have you ever experienced in your life that you attracted something that you wanted? How did it happen? What did you learn?

Chapter 9

LEARNING TO
LET GO AND FORGIVE

*When true forgiveness happens it is one of the most astonishing and
liberating of the human experiences.*
—Richard Holloway

I continued working for Robert and went back and forth to
Mullingstorp to help out as a volunteering assistant, in order to
learn more about health and personal self-development. Robert
decided to move from Richmond Hill, London, to Monte Carlo,
Monaco, a place that carried heavy memories for me. So even though it
was very glamorous and exciting, it was hard at the same time.

In 1997, I moved from my small studio to a bigger apartment in the suburb of Stockholm, so Robert could come and stay with me when he came to visit in Sweden, since he didn't have a place of his own.

One day after Robert came back from one of the courses at Mullingstorp, I noticed he had a necklace around his neck. I asked what it was, and he said a girl at the course gave it to him. I was very inquisitive and had a bad feeling in my stomach. He seemed so high and happy. He later, without even a sense of compassion, told me that he liked her and that he thought we needed to give our relationship a break. I could not believe my ears! I had just moved to the bigger apartment! What a jerk! He had the bad manners to break up with me? I was devastated. It was just the second time in my life somebody broke up with me. I fell into a big hole of misery. My dad had to come to the rescue, and as he comforted me, all night long, we drank the whiskey that he had brought with him.

I had just no idea how to sustain myself in the new setting. We stopped working together so now I didn't have a boyfriend nor a job. My friend Sandy suggested that I take Lomi Lomi massage training in Hawaii. I had no idea how to get there and how to afford it, but I did have the expensive Ebel watch. And since Robert had left me, I vengefully took it to the pawnshop. It covered the trip and the training. It was a beautiful experience, but I was so desperate looking for love and approval. I had a crush on the massage teacher and had a short affair with him. When I came back, I had to work hard. I started to work at a gym in Stockholm as a massage therapist and teaching meditation.

I rented out a room in my apartment to a friend of mine who was a great photographer and had taken some of my model shots in the early 1990s. He needed a place to stay since his girlfriend kicked him out, so it was a perfect fit. At least I thought so at first. I felt sorry for him and wanted to help. It turned out it wasn't a great idea since he needed professional help. His girlfriend was physically abusing him, and he was more or less depressed and sat in front of his computer all day. I finally succeeded in getting rid of the apartment and moved to downtown Stockholm into a smaller flat. The day I was moving, the photographer was still in his room. He had not packed a thing. He simply had nowhere to go, so he was more or less pushed out when the new renters came to move in. They were, of course, furious, and it was most embarrassing, since I was the responsible person. He succeeded in moving into a friend's office, and I ended up being his "therapist," which wasn't a good idea. When I finally put my foot down and told him that I was tired of playing his psychologist, he stopped harassing me, and I have not heard from him since. I learned that sometimes when you think you are helping someone you are actually not, but rather inhibiting him or her from moving forward.

Robert called me a few months later asking me how I was. He told me about his life and since we have always been very open with each other he told me a few things that triggered the memories of him leaving me a few months earlier. It was hard to listen to all of it. He also told me that it hadn't worked out with his new girlfriend and that he had broken up with her. I felt pretty good about that!

He said he was going to play at the US Open in San Francisco, and what he said next I would never forget, "I need some female energy. Can you come?"

I was shocked. I thought, *What the hell! Am I suddenly good enough for him?* I was in turmoil inside. "What the heck, Robert!" I said. "If you really want me, you better come on a white horse and ask for me!" And that was that! I was still hurting so much, and at the same time I was flattered that he called and asked. But heck no! I wasn't going to be some darn female energy to fulfill his needs.

One week later the doorbell rang and outside was the most the beautiful bouquet of red roses being delivered with a note from Robert:

I'm sorry, I don't have a white horse but can you please consider coming? I will pay for everything.

The tournament was in San Francisco, a city I was curious about. And, while there, I was going to also spend time with and learn from Bengt and Bengt's girlfriend Victoria. I thought, *What the heck, I will go! What's the worst thing that can happen?*

When I arrived in San Francisco and saw Robert, the feelings I still had for him took over, and even though the pride within me wanted to fight for my honor, I completely surrendered into his strong arms, and was swept away by the forces of nature.

UGH! I didn't like that my love and longing for him took over rather than waiting for him to show me first that he was—not only interested in having sex—but also interested in me as a person. I would have liked to be cooler, letting him work for it more before letting him back in. During that trip, it became pretty clear that we were becoming a couple again, but it was still a lot for me to heal.

Have you ever experienced being betrayed? Have you healed, or are you still holding grudges? What did you do to learn from the incident? How can your experience help you move forward in your life?

Chapter 10

I Am the Creator
of My Own Reality

Imagination is everything. It is the preview of life's coming attractions.
—Albert Einstein

We went back to work together on tour, and we were getting closer and closer, and in 1999, we decided to buy a vacation home in Sweden. A very nice man, Mats, a manager at IMG, Stockholm, The International Managing Group, that managed Robert's business, had been looking for a house for us for a while when he saw an ad in the paper. It seemed to be a beautiful villa outside Stockholm, in the countryside, conveniently located close to the International airport, Arlanda.

We both agreed on going there to look at it. I had a really good feeling about it. It was a beautiful spring day, and it was situated in a small village. It was very different. When we came down the driveway and saw the house, lo and behold, it was remarkably close to the house I had drawn on the picture with my mom while doing the vision quest a few years earlier. I knew this was the house for us. The house was called Villa Phantasia, and it was painted in blue, facing lake Mälaren on a lovely green lot. As we rang the doorbell, I was filled with excitement. A man in his late 40s opened the door dressed in white. He was warm and welcoming. His name was Jonas. He welcomed us in to show us the house and just around the corner came another man. Jonas introduced him as his good friend Peter. I could not believe my eyes. To my great surprise, it was my old meditation teacher, who had taught my family and me to meditate many years ago.

It turned out we had come to the Transcendental Meditation Village: The Ideal Village that Peter had told us about, the one that my family and I had looked into being a part of several years earlier. We ended up buying the house!

Did you ever have any experience of creating your reality? Our have you experienced similar kinds of synchronicity?

Chapter 11

What You Do Unto Others
Shall Be Done unto You

Someone told me the delightful story of the crusader who put a chastity belt on his wife and gave the key to his best friend for safekeeping, in case of his death. He had ridden only a few miles away when his friend, riding hard, caught up with him, saying "You gave me the wrong key!"

—Anaïs Nin

I n the fall of 2000, I started a therapist training in Denmark as part of pursuing my education. I went there every six weeks for over one and a half years. During that time, we renovated the vacation home and made it what we wanted to make it.

Robert was gone a lot on tour, so I focused on my education. During my training I met a man who worked as a therapist. He was very handsome and attractive. He showed me a lot of the appreciation that I was so hungry for and that I felt I didn't get from Robert. During one workshop we became very close and I developed some emotions for him and told Robert that I wanted to go and see him.

He was fine with it, and I went. When I got to his place he was so charming and romantic that it was so hard to resist him. I ended up going to bed with him.

The following day I traveled back home. I felt horrible. How could I betray Robert in such a horrible way? He had trust in me, and I let him down. We had agreed on meeting at his parents' house, since Robert was in the area anyway. His mom met me at the door, and when she looked at me and asked how I was, I felt so ashamed. I immediately started to tell her that I had done something really bad and that Robert was going to be upset with me. She told me not to worry. Later in the car when we drove back to our place, I told him the truth. He was very upset. He broke up with me.

I only had a small company working from home with biofeedback, massage, and meditation. I had very little income. I was terrified. And I still loved Robert very much.

I begged and begged for him to give me a second chance. He finally agreed to it, and said ok. I worked very hard on showing my appreciation. But I had not dealt with the all the pain inside of me, and I was still very jealous and afraid of being hurt again. Once his old love from Mullingstorp came to visit. Since he wanted to see her, I tried to be strong and said it was fine. After all I had very little right to say no, considering what I had done to him. They were gone for hours, and I started becoming very nervous. I started imagining that they would have sex in the car and that he wanted her back and all kinds of nasty stuff. By the time they came back several hours had passed, and I had not heard from him. I was so wound up that I had to hold myself back from killing the poor girl. As they entered the hallway, I shouted, "Where have you been, and what the heck have you done?" They both looked shocked and nervous. Robert immediately told me off and to calm down, and quickly said goodbye to the girl. I felt so hurt even though it turned out they had only been out on a walk. I was clearly not as strong as I had hoped for. I felt a lot of old unhealed pain from the past pouring out; How could he just leave me there without even calling me letting me know what was going on? He was furious with me and thought that I was very insulting to her. I thought that I had made a point: This was my man. She is a slut, and she must be put in place. I was clearly projecting my own fear and insecurities onto her.

There was still a lot of pain that needed to be healed between us. We knew we had to do something to make it better. My family's friend and coach, Sandy, suggested that Robert and I take part in a couples' course based on Tantra, led by an American couple, Light and Brian Miller, the kindest and sweetest couple. Tantra is a Sanskrit word meaning, "weaving." It originated in ancient Hindu and Buddhist cultures of India and Tibet, and consists of teachings and practices. It's mainly about accepting and connecting, weaving everything together as being part of a divine manifestation.

By consciously uniting perceived opposites (male and female, light and dark) human beings can transcend dualism and know that all is one. Tantra weaves together sensuality and spirit. The goal of Tantra is to allow us to experience more depth and breadth in every aspect of our daily lives. A Tantric experience is not a sexual practice as many people seem to think but a highly spiritual practice and involves conscious breathing, muscle contraction exercises, sound, visualization, meditation, sensual touch, creating a sacred, loving space, and sacred spiritual rituals. The goal is increased awareness leading to greater understanding of ourselves.

The training was life-changing since we shifted our sexual energy to move from sex to love and it was deeply healing for both of us. It opened up a whole new world for us where we finally started to reconnect on a more spiritual level.

Shortly after that, I became pregnant with our first child—our daughter, Thea.

Tantra, or weaving the energies, can be a great way of coming together from any kind of sexual abuse, or betrayal.

If you, like me, did betray anyone, you know how the guilt can eat you up from the inside. The most difficult and frightening thing is to tell the truth. The truth will set you free. And that is what it did to me. I'd rather live alone than live in a lie. So in a sense, it was easy to tell the truth.

If you had a chance to relive your life would you still relive the same experience and cheat and betray another person? If not, why? What was it that you were looking for that made you cheat or betray the person? What was the greatest lesson that you learned?

Chapter 12

THERE IS NO SUCH THING AS DEATH

Never. We never lose our loved ones. They accompany us; they don't disappear from our lives. We are merely in different rooms.
—Paulo Coelho, Aleph

I n the spring of 2000, Robert and I had done a three-week long detox and fasting at Mullingstorp together with some other participants. We were on a strict diet of milk and bread following Dr. Koyer from Austria. His studies were remarkable, and many people had been cured of all kinds of diseases just by fasting and letting the intestines rest. He was also performing some massage that rejuvenates and calms the whole gut system. And he could tell you who you were just by looking at your body constitution. He told me very quickly that I needed to stop worrying, if I wanted to stay healthy, since he noticed how much energy I spent on worrying about things.

We were very fortunate to have this opportunity to spend time with Dr. Koyer, since he was a very old man and he passed away not long after our time together.

I came in contact with a lot of interesting healing techniques while working as an assistant with Dr. Bengt Stern at Mullingstorp. As part of healing and growing, we invited our parents to go on the course with us on our personal growth journey.

My parents had great experiences, and were rejuvenated by going there. Robert's mom was the sweetest, but she was very much holding back what she felt inside and wasn't very expressive.

Summer 2001, she got sick. She wasn't diagnosed until the disease was far gone. She had sarcoma in the diaphragm. With our experience over the past few years working with Mullingstorp, we thought it was a good idea for her to try alternative methods, as Dr. Stern himself was diagnosed with lymphoma and had survived long past his expected survival time. She didn't want to; she wanted to go the conventional route.

A couple of months earlier we had found out that I was pregnant, and I knew inside of me that it was a girl but didn't want to do the test to find out since it really didn't matter to us. Valborg, Robert's mom, was so happy for us and had started knitting little sweaters and hats for the baby. We had just returned from taking the ultrasound at the hospital, but before for leaving for Scotland, Robert called his dad Björn, to check out how things were in general. Straight away Björn told him, "It is not good. The doctors gave up hope on your mom's survival yesterday. From now on, they are just trying to make her last few days as bearable as possible." We did not know that she had two surgeries that were unsuccessful and made the cancer grow much quicker. Now it was just a matter of time.

We dropped everything and went to the hospital in a heartbeat. When we came up to her room, she was in bed and looked very weak, but she smiled when we came, and we showed her the little ultrasound photo of the baby. She was very moved when I put her hand on my stomach as she connected with the baby. She smiled and looked happy as she gave me the little knitted garments that she had been knitting so lovingly. I was so moved by her love, tears filled my eyes, and I couldn't hold my tears back. Robert and I stayed with her during the days that week, and I could sense that she didn't want to die. She really wanted to be there when the baby would arrive. She struggled for several days with the fact that she was so weak and probably wouldn't survive. Watching her struggle was very painful. I could tell she was going back and forth over the last couple of days, as she seemed to leave her body and come back into it. When I saw how peace finally filled her face, I knew that the time had come and she surrendered to the fact that she was leaving this life. Instantly I felt her presence. More than I had ever felt any living human being. Her presence was literally a part of me. I then knew in my heart and soul that there is no such thing as death. On Thursday night, we stayed over in the bedroom next to her cramped up in the hospital bed.

The following morning, Björn must have felt what was going on and asked us to leave so that Robert's sister would get a chance to come and say farewell on her own. He said he would call us as soon as something changed. That evening at 8 we got the phone call. She had transferred to the other side. The days at the hospital were some of the most beautiful and profound experiences in my life. Since that day, I have sensed her presence many times. In my opinion, death is simply a transition. We are simply leaving our tool, our body, our temple, in this third dimension, and the soul goes back to where it came from.

As I grew up as a Christian, I was never taught about reincarnation until I went to school and learned about different religions but of course also from my parents' experiences and from books that they had read about life after death, e.g., the book *On Death and Dying* by Elisabeth Kubler Ross. As a teenager, Reincarnation was to me the most natural thing; we would surely come back to this planet somehow. Now I have come to believe that it is not certain we are reincarnated on this planet, we might go somewhere else, depending on our choices.

A couple of years ago, I took part of a drum journey ceremony. It was a guided meditation where the guide used drums to put the participants in a trance-like state. I then experienced—like a lucid dream –traveling between dimensions and flying on top of an eagle into the sun. I was surprised at first since I thought we would burn getting too close, but instead we entered another reality. It was a place full of human beings in energy form that were waiting to go somewhere else. The sun was like a waiting place, where we would connect and meet and wait to go somewhere else, maybe back to earth or somewhere else in the universe.

Have you ever experienced death? Do you have or know someone who has lost a dear one? What was it like for you? What are your thoughts concerning death and what do you think will happen when it's your time to leave? What would you have liked to accomplish before you leave this planet?

Chapter 13

THAT I DIDN'T
DIE GIVING BIRTH

In giving birth to our babies, we may find that we give birth to new possibilities within ourselves.

—Jon Kabat-Zinn

Being pregnant was absolutely amazing as well as a very challenging thing, especially since I didn't get a lot of support from Robert, who was gone a lot, or from my mom.

As part of being a stubborn and independent woman, and probably a bit fearful to be left again and not being able to sustain myself, I started to study medicine and feng shui, to incorporate into my business. But as the pregnancy proceeded, I didn't have the energy to complete the studies, and I felt like a failure again. So what I focused on and insisted on was to have a natural birth with no chemicals or medical procedures. I practiced breathing, yoga, and did everything according to the most recent studies on how to deliver a baby the natural way, and in my opinion at that time, the healthy way. I ate healthily, I used aromatherapy, and I was very judgmental to mothers who seemed to trust conventional medicine. By the middle December of 2001, I was two weeks overdue and huge. We left for the hospital on the 17th. I had a tough birth with Thea, our daughter, as I was insisting on doing it naturally and fought to the bitter end like the real wild boar that I was. I was ready to kill Robert, who I felt was in the way. He had no understanding whatsoever of what I was going through as he told me to "Stop whining and cut out the complaining," especially the first day.

After 40 hours or so, he wasn't so tough anymore and started to understand that he was going to have a baby and that I was in a lot of pain. I was so done and had not slept at all, and to my disappointment, I had to take an epidural, which then slowed the whole process down.

After 48 hours on Wednesday morning on the 19th, I had to have an episiotomy so that they could drag Thea out since she was stuck. Thea was very blue and did not breathe. She was briefly put on my stomach, and I was told it was serious. But inside of me I sensed she was fine. As soon as they cut the cord, the doctor told Robert to follow instantly to the emergency room. Thea was still not breathing. When Robert came out into the corridor the doctors were already gone and he had to find his way to the emergency room. When he opened the door, he saw the doctors shoving a tube down her tiny throat to cleanse the airways. He freaked out as, in his mind, he thought the tube was longer than her. After some suction, she finally coughed, and he could hear her weak voice squeaking. They came back in the room with her, and that's when I saw the light turn on in Robert's eyes for the first time as he held his new born child. He was a proud father. I learned that I had been very judgmental and had I had the birth my way, Thea might not have been alive. I was most grateful to conventional medicine that day. But if it hadn't been for all the preparation I had done I would never had lasted that long, 48 hours without sleep and breathing through contractions, without being able to push since I was not open enough, for over 1.5 hours, was impressive, at least the midwives seemed to think so. And it made me heal quicker and I knew I was much stronger than I've ever been.

That Christmas Robert was responsible for any Christmas decorations. Since he usually didn't care much about it, it was usually up to me to decorate. I completely surrendered into motherhood, and I spent my time pointing at the Christmas tree, telling Robert where to put the decorations since I couldn't sit or hardly walk. I had a huge, golf-ball-sized hematoma between my legs after the cut they did to pull Thea out. When she was five weeks old, I put her in the stroller and left for the airport. I had a plane to Australia to catch. Robert had been gone for a couple weeks practicing and was gladly anticipating seeing his family.

Have you given birth? How was it? What did you learn? If you have not, is it something you would like to do? Why? How would you like it to be? I think writing down what we would like the experience to be could be very useful. I never thought it would be as painful as it was, and I think it could have helped me to go through different scenarios in my head and not only the perfect picture of the perfect birth in my mind.

Chapter 14

INNER STRENGTH

Birth is not only about making babies. Birth is about making mothers—strong, competent, capable mothers who trust themselves and know their inner strength.

—**Barbara Katz Rothman**

One of the hardest trips that I ever have done was when I went to see Robert that time. I had just come out of the first 13-hour flight with Thea to transfer in Singapore. I was exhausted and had not slept much since much of my energy went to making sure Thea didn't wake any passengers up. She was a quiet baby, so it worked out well. I was just about to enter the Singapore airlines flight to Perth when the flight attendant looked at my passport and said,

"You don't have a Visa?" "What do you mean?" I answered. "Yes, you are clearly missing your visa and can't board the flight." I was confused and shocked. *What do I do now?* Luckily my cell phone was charged, so I started calling our manager at IMG, The International Managing Group that was Robert's managing group at that time, and it turned out they had never fixed the visa for me, but they said that they would look into it a.s.a.p. The visa was sorted out electronically, and we could board the next flight 6 hours later. During the wait I was tired and smelled of sweat and breastmilk, trying to get some rest on a hard bench in the airport. Thea seemed comfortable and nursed as usual. I was relieved to finally get on the plane and tried to get some sleep, but it wasn't so easy since she then decided to be awake!

Nine hours later I landed in Perth. I was glad to be there, but I was exhausted. When I was finally getting the stroller out to put Thea in it, it was broken, and, since it had been sent in cargo, it was dirty as well. I had to carry her and the luggage through customs. Robert came and met us. I was in a very bad mood! I was super-exhausted, and I just wanted to hand the baby over to him and go on vacation. The first thing he asked was, "What's wrong with you? Why are you so grumpy?" I literally wanted to kill him and then lie down and cry. I struggled many times being a mother and not feeling that I had support from him. He seemed so uninterested, and it was hard for me to understand why he wasn't there for Thea and me. He was, of course, feeling more pressure to perform now as he was a father and needed to step up to the plate and support his family.

Since he was almost never home, and I was desperate to get some help, we decided to get a nanny. It was a wise choice but even though I was very grateful to all the sweet girls that have helped us on the journey, having a nanny wasn't always easy for me.

I struggled between wanting to be in control and being the perfect mom who could do everything on her own. I didn't know anyone of my

Swedish friends who had nannies. It was only on the golf circuit that I would encounter women who travelled alone while their kids were at home with their nannies. Before I had kids I was very judgmental and thought they were simply "bad" moms and it wasn't until I had kids myself and realized how important they came to be for me that I finally understood.

Living with another woman in my house also became a challenge since I was often afraid that Robert would like them more than me, and of course, he is a man and wanted to look at women, especially young beautiful ones, something that freaked me out since it reminded me of my father and his behavior. I also struggled with asking for private time with Robert, something I desperately needed, since he was away a lot, but then that would mean I would have had to show my weakness as I thought, so I kept it to myself. It was not until later that I began to understand Robert and that being on tour all the time surrounded by men, having women around was an uplifting thing for him. To me it became an internal fight. I wanted to be the strong wife who could share my husband but at the same time I craved his attention and longed to be the only one. I started feeling more and more confused. I didn't travel as much with Robert, and when he got home, I felt like he always seemed more interested in spending time in front of the TV or talking to the nannies, than spending time with me. I had huge expectations of him; I wanted him to take over the household chores, help me and give me what I thought I deserved. And my expectations proved right. I was entirely acting out of projecting my own lack of self –love and got what I focused on: no attention whatsoever. Sure we had sex, and that was fine, but I wanted to feel loved, to be the only one, to be adored and honored. It never hit me that he was tired and exhausted and just needed to be. Working as a High Performer he had enough of pressures on himself as it was and didn't need more pressure from me. I was very self- focused.

Since I was so busy with the baby, he probably felt left out as well, as many men do and I didn't give him the attention that he was hoping for and was used to before parenthood.

I found myself stuck at home more and more, redoing it and making it beautiful. I thought by fixing things on the outside I would feel better. In reality, this was only half the truth. What I actually wanted was to fix myself, my inside, and make that be beautiful.

Osho, the Indian guru, whose teachings I followed for many years, so often said wise things. One of the things he said that really made an impact on me was this: "It's not a beautiful house, it's a beautiful you." How true are those words? We so often struggle so hard to fix the outside world. How much energy, time, and money does it take, and for what reason? I have moved about 10 times in the last 16 years, and now I finally have started to surrender to that thought. I love to make things beautiful, but I simply have embraced the fact that I can't be everywhere at the same time and I can't do it all at once. And it's ok.

Nowadays I'm mainly focusing on my internal beauty: accepting and loving myself as well as being aware of my thoughts, actions, and emotions. Robert told me something recently over Facetime while he was on one of his trips. Looking at me in my scruffy outfit, my not-so-done hairdo, and my sloppy weekend make-up, he told me that I was more beautiful than ever. I wanted to cry happy tears. The truth is, beauty is also in the eyes of the beholder and he can always choose to see my true beauty.

Being a frequent flyer mom, I learned early on that the more nervous I was about the baby starting to cry during the flight, the more likely it was that it was going to happen. That's how the Law of Attraction works. And if we as parents will just relax more and let the baby nurse on the breast or bottle while taking off and landing, the baby will be more content. I learned that it was important to take care of myself to be a happy mom in order to have happy kids. So on my long trips, I would ask the staff if they could help me out with carrying the baby if I needed to get some rest. It worked all the time.

There were of course some great benefits from having a nanny, besides the friendship that I would develop with them it also gave me a lot of freedom to travel and do other things that simply wouldn't have been possible without them. On one of the trips to South America, Thea was less than a year old and I went away for three weeks. The coach I had at the time would ask me to let go of any emotions and worry regarding the trip. To my great surprise Thea didn't ask for me once or cry for me and when I got back she gave me a hug like nothing had happened. Learning how to trust another person and allowing them to take responsibility for the most precious thing in my life, made me realize how I had taken ownership of my children and made myself invaluable. Later in life this made the children more flexible and not so demanding.

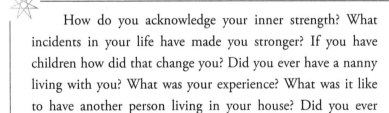

How do you acknowledge your inner strength? What incidents in your life have made you stronger? If you have children how did that change you? Did you ever have a nanny living with you? What was your experience? What was it like to have another person living in your house? Did you ever compromise with your feelings?

Chapter 15

A New Inspiration

When the student is ready, the teacher will appear.
—Buddha

O ne fall evening in October, my friend Mia called and wondered if she could come and stay with Robert and me. She told me she had started working with a Swedish lady. I told her how hard it was being a mom and being on my own a lot of the time. I explained how much I had studied all kinds of techniques to feel better. She told me, "Ebba, you don't have to look for the answers outside of yourself. You have them all within." And as she said that I felt relieved, but at the same time disappointed: then would I have to let go of being a seeker, since to be a seeker, you keep looking for the truth?

And in one second, all my seeking seemed in vain: all the books, all the courses, and all the trainings. *Was it all in vain? Unnecessary?* She continued and told me that her friend was a businesswoman who had discovered how she could communicate with her inner self, how to ask questions and how to get the answers from herself. I was mesmerized, and I wanted to meet her. I got my chance and it was a fascinating meeting; She was a warm and loving woman who seemed fearless; her ideas turned my world upside down. She had a way of putting everything I had learned spiritually into perspective, and also of questioning the stuff I had learned. It was challenging and interesting. And as I embraced the ideas, I thought that they were very refreshing and liberating. I started clearing my life from the spiritual stuff I had been collecting through the years, the stuff that I had clung to, and that I thought was my identity. I was able to start fresh and anew. I chose to stop reading spiritual and self-help books, got rid of them and other spiritual objects and stuffed my old tarot cards away, so that I could start asking myself the questions and finding out things within myself.

Later on, I was even more uplifted by her insights, and we decided to hold a workshop where we lived to share our new insights. I started marketing the workshop, and as soon as we did that, people started to show a significant interest. We had a fairly successful workshop in our vacation home. Both Robert and I were excited about the concept, and during that spring, Robert asked Mia's friend if she could become his coach and help him with his golf. She became his coach and to protect her identity I am calling her the coach.

We took part in several other workshops and decided that it was something we wanted to work with ourselves. The coach lived in Luleå, the northern parts of Sweden, and we travelled there several times to visit her. Later we met some other people, mostly business people with different backgrounds and together we decided to develop a concept for personal leadership. The idea was to start working together to build a business network working with developing personal leadership tools and to create a foundation. We were about a dozen businesspersons from Sweden and Norway that came together to start up the project. We decided to start the foundation in the village with great infrastructure situated by the Luleå river, by the Arctic Circle in Lapland. It was a place where the sun never set in the summer and where in the winter, the snow was white and crisp like a fairytale. We often saw reindeer roaming around and met Sami people who still work with breeding and herding them.

By the fall of 2003, I found out that I was pregnant with our second child and we decided to sell our vacation home in the Ideal Village and have the vacation home in Lapland instead, since we spent a lot of time there. This was a challenging time of my life since Thea was only 2. I was hesitant to move since it was so far away from my parents and I really needed their support as a young mom, even though my mom was never really supportive in the way I wanted.

My longing for internal freedom was stronger than the fear of letting go of my "comfort zone", and by the summer of 2004, I decided to leave Monaco for a while and flew seven months pregnant to Lapland to give birth to the baby and create a fresh start. Robert was on tour but would join me when it was time to deliver the baby. I left my dream vacation home that I had been working on for over five years, and we bought an older house that was in need of renovation, half the size of the house in Stockholm.

By the time I was due to deliver the baby, it was far different from the birth of Thea, our first child. This time I had the coach with me and she was amazing. She told me to focus on the breathing and encouraged me to find my inner strength. I was able to deliver the baby in just 7 hours and without any medicinal support besides breathing in some "laughing" gas. Out came the most perfect little boy without any complications.

It was hard to move to Lapland even though there were many helpful people that assisted me. The people of the village were genuine and very friendly. I had never before in my life experienced so much unconditional love from strangers. People offered their help and came over with food while I was unpacking from the move. It was a very open, safe, and caring society and a great place to have a family. The combination of living in Monaco and having a vacation home in Lapland was a beautiful choice for our family since our kids could get the best of two worlds.

By the time the moving truck came with all our stuff, I was exhausted. Robert was out on tour golfing and Ceasar, our son, was just a month old or so, when 300 boxes and our furniture arrived to be squeezed into the much smaller vacation home. I sat frozen with Ceasar in my arms on the beautiful sofa that I just had upholstered to fit the colorful living room in the old house. It filled up the whole living room in the new house and most of furniture didn't fit the new abode. There was simply no place to walk or move. There was stuff everywhere! I sat down and cried. I thought, *Why did I move here?* I missed my old house and my mom terribly. We realized we needed to expand and renovate the vacation home. The coach came to the rescue. She had also bought a house in the village and the renovation of it was just finished. She offered us the chance to get away from living in the midst of a construction site. Instead she generously offered for us to move into her newly renovated home, while she moved out to a small side building without water, a toilet and shower possibilities, during the time we renovated and extended the house. It was an irresistible offer, and we gratefully said yes. The house turned out beautifully after the renovation, and we could move in after six months.

Moving is a great opportunity to let go of material belongings that we think we need, as the things we own often reflect our personality, and by shedding ourselves from stuff we can more easily find our true value. We often measure our value by the things we own and the money we have in the bank. Today I know that worldly stuff never leads to lasting happiness.

Have you ever let go of beliefs that you thought was your truth? Have you ever let go of a house that you thought was your everything; your life, your future, and your investment? If so, what did you experience? How was it for you to leave behind what you thought was a part of you? What insights did you gain?

Chapter 16

PERSPECTIVE ON THE MEDIA

Whoever controls the media, controls the mind.
—Jim Morrison

The time we spent in Lapland was refreshing. It was fun to be part of a network and to share the same interest in growing together. Life in Monaco was more geared towards servicing the self and I had not found a sense of community there. It was fun to get to know and work together with many of the villagers, in Lapland, starting up several businesses, renovating houses, including developing personal leadership tools for our common business. As I brought those tools and insights with me back to Monaco I could also work from there.

The media found out that Robert and I had started to work with a network of people that wanted to do something different. And like happens so very often, the media wanted to create a story that would increase their sales in my opinion, so they drew parallels with another story that just had happened in small a community in the south of Sweden, that was cult-related. Personal leadership was, back in those days, something unusual and some people thought it was strange. It didn't matter that what we worked to develop was based on common-sense knowledge and living out of personal leadership. It all broke loose when a famous documentary TV show in Sweden contacted us to do some interviews and to find out about us and what we were working with. We were very willing to assist them and answered all their questions, trusting that they were going to present our business and ourselves fairly. But oh, so wrong we were! When the documentary came out, we were shocked: They had just pretended to be very interested in the concept and instead of reporting the truth, made up a horrible story to get more viewers.

The whole incident is kind of amusing, since the story that the media presented was the total opposite of what I took part in developing. The Personal Leadership tools were based on common sense and the ideas that: We always have a choice how to approach any given situation, we are all connected, we all have equal value, and we are all good deep down inside.

It was great stuff that we wanted to share in seminar form: how we can create more peace within and take personal leadership in everyday life. It was all about taking ownership of one's own actions, reactions, and emotions. It was about not blaming anybody for anything, but taking back one's own power in one's life

I volunteered, with others in the village, to help start up several organizations and businesses, for the survival of the village. This was also an important part of my own growth since I had been very self-focused earlier in my life. Volunteering helped me realize that to be in service to others was something that I benefited from as well.

It was a fascinating time, since the network had decided to give each other assistance to grow. That was how the leadership tools developed. At the same time, it was very challenging, as we needed to be introspective and look at our own patterns individually.

We had amazing results in our individual lives and wanted to be more scientific, so we took the chance and worked with Princeton University to see if the work we did could be measurable.

We teamed up with The Global Consciousness Project (GCP), created originally in the Princeton Engineering Anomalies Research Lab at Princeton University, with the director, Roger Nelson. The Institute of Noetic Sciences provides a logistical home for the GCP.

The Global Consciousness Project is explained here from the site: **www.noospehere.princeton.edu**

Coherent consciousness creates order in the world
Subtle interactions link us with each other and the Earth
When human consciousness becomes coherent, the behavior of random systems may change. Random number generators (RNGs) based on quantum tunneling produce completely unpredictable sequences of zeroes and ones. But when a great event synchronizes the feelings of millions of people, our network of RNGs becomes subtly structured. We calculate one in a trillion odds that the effect is due to chance. The evidence suggests an emerging noosphere or the unifying field of consciousness described by sages in all cultures.

The Global Consciousness Project is an international, multidisciplinary collaboration of scientists and engineers. We collect data continuously from a global network of physical random number generators located in up to 70 host sites around the world at any given time. The data are transmitted to a central archive

*which now contains more than 15 years of random data in parallel
sequences of synchronized 200-bit trials generated every second.*

*Our purpose is to examine subtle correlations that may
reflect the presence and activity of consciousness in the world. We
hypothesize that there will be a structure in what should be random
data, associated with major global events that engage our minds
and hearts.*

*Subtle but real effects of consciousness are important scientifically,
but their real power is more immediate. They encourage us to make
essential, healthy changes in the great systems that dominate our
world. Large-scale group consciousness has effects in the physical
world. Knowing this, we can intentionally work toward a brighter,
more conscious future.*

Obviously, after the documentary was broadcasted, it was challenging
to deal with all the false rumors. People who didn't know us sometimes
behaved in a very negative way, and had horrible things to say without
even knowing the facts. We did however get a lot of practice in staying
centered and not choosing to be affected by things going on outside,
thanks to our individual personal leadership.

It became very apparent to me that a lot of people listen to media,
and believe in what is presented as the truth. They can, therefore, be
easily misled, believing in things they are told without questioning the
facts and the origin of the story.

This phenomenon became even clearer when I visited an expo, years
later at the Holocaust museum in Washington, D.C., about Hitler's
propaganda machine and how he so successfully manipulated a whole
country. Through these experiences, I have been more careful about
believing what the media is presenting in general. I know it's crucial
that people are critical thinkers and question what they see and hear.
In my opinion, the best way to identify false information is to learn to

trust your inner knowing. And with that I mean the inner knowledge that we have with us coming into this world, the knowledge from the soul that is connected to source, the one, and the universe, God. It's not the taught knowledge we gain from reading and learning. In my opinion, we are living in a society where people are being dumbed down by not being taught from early age how to listen to and trust their inner knowing. Without this experience with the media, I would probably not have developed this interest: to find the source of the fact. I know today that 90% of the media in the US is controlled by six corporations. It looks the same all over the world. Even in Sweden, the media is severely controlled, mainly by two big corporations, their power, if they wanted to use it, could have enormous consequences.

How do you cultivate a freethinking mind? Do you question what you see and hear in the media or do you take it as the truth? What do you think you can do to become more knowledgeable? What can you do to increase your critical thinking? How can you develop your inner knowing?

Chapter 17

BREAKING THROUGH CONDITIONING

The only way of finding the limits of the possible is by going beyond them into the impossible.
—Arthur C. Clarke

R obert worked very closely with the coach, and he played really well. He raced up the ranking lists and played more events out of Europe. I was so happy for him and for us. But at the same time, I felt like he spent more time with the coach and the people in the network when we were in Sweden, and not with the kids and me. I struggled with feeling alone, and started to become very jealous. I wanted to keep his time and focus to myself. Of course,

I didn't know then that the more I focused on the lack of having him around, the more I created that situation and actually maybe even pushed him away.

I started to work more intensely with the coach as well, trying to deal with my issues. She felt that she could help me feel better which would also help Robert in the long run. And yes, she did help me appreciate the small things in life, being in the moment while cooking, hanging the laundry, etc., making it more fun and enjoyable. I was more often content with the situation. I succeeded in breaking through a lot of the victimhood that I had so long identified with.

Thanks to her assistance I chose to release a lot of old baggage that I had carried around with me for a long time. I became a lot more unselfish, thinking more about others' needs, expanding my vision and the impact my choices could have on others around me. Yet, there were many things that I really struggled with. My life became a rollercoaster of emotions.

After working on breaking through my illusions and conditionings, I could one day experience a feeling of being so high on life that I was on top of the world and the next I would drop down into a pit hole of misery. I found myself then being very depressed by the whole situation, especially in my relationship with Robert. I often felt that the only thing he wanted from me was sex and to have a clean house to come home to, and of course food on the table. I ended up feeling like a housemaid and a prostitute rather than a partner and a wife. Unfortunately, that became the only way for me to feel his love, and many times I had sex with him without even really wanting it. I just wanted to feel that he loved me, and I wanted to please him. This usually backlashed since deep inside I was furious at myself for not standing up for myself and being honest about my feelings.

Thanks to the assistance from the coach, Robert started to open up and become a much more caring person to me but also to other people.

This was great, but I also struggled with it since I really wanted him for myself, especially since he was already gone so much, and I didn't feel like I was important to him. The work we did with personal leadership meant that we would come a lot closer to each other, as he stretched himself out of his previous comfort zone, and expanded his vision, becoming more of himself and growing more as a person. He opened up sides that neither of us had seen in him before. He had been pretty held back before, more quiet and shy. Now he became more open, more courageous, and more secure in himself. It started igniting a lust within him, and like many men, he went too far.

As he had grown up in a fairly safe environment—mainly focusing on sports as a young man—this newly awakened energy within him made him want to explore life more. He made several bad choices when it came to women. It was very painful, especially since it involved a few women I knew and was very close to. I felt it, I dreamed about it, and my intuition mixed with my fear of being betrayed. It was a vicious circle. I'm sure I had a great part in creating the whole scenario. Since I had been exploring that part of myself as a young woman, there was no reason to do it now that I was married to Robert. I understand that being on the road, on tour as a man, is a very difficult thing, and it's easy to fall for temptation. When Robert started to play well, his confidence rose, and he dared to do things he had not done before. Unfortunately, this had a lot of bad consequences for our relationship.

I felt something was going on for some time, but didn't know what it was, since I felt so jealous, the last thing I wanted to do was to have sex with him when he came home. I wanted him to suffer the way I did. Since I was often very tired taking care of the kids and the house, I also used that as an excuse for not having the will to have sex. I felt like he had very little understanding for me and what I was going through, I felt that it was always about him and how I could best support him. It didn't help that I so often got the message from the people working with him—be it the caddy, physiotherapist, or golf coach—that I needed to care for him so that he could perform better. The coach would ask me to take care of my own emotions and stop projecting my misery on him. It was true. I did project my frustration. I felt very alone in parenting. I so wanted him to be the father that I never had. We moved six times within Monaco, and not once did Robert help me much. I was the boss of the household and found myself in a life situation that I didn't really dig! As Robert shared what he felt on and off the golf course with the coach, I felt that he didn't speak as much as I wanted him to with me, and I felt even more on the outside.

Maybe it was because we started to drift apart from each other that Robert did what he did, or maybe there was a combination of several things.

One day, Robert decided to face his fears and, with the support of the coach, told me the truth about his side steps. All the pain that had been built up for so long within me exploded and as soon as I heard the details of what had happened, my right hand quickly moved to my fourth finger on the left hand. I pulled the wedding ring off in a flash and threw it on the table. I screamed, and I started shaking and crying at the same time. "That's it," I said, "I'm out of here," and I stood up. The coach tried to calm me down and told me to breathe slowly and to sit down. Robert looked shocked and scared.

After some long conversations, we decided to stay together and work through it. I felt like the worst piece of crap in the world, I felt so betrayed. Even with that in mind, I was ready to try to make it work. There was a part of me that understood that he had never played around as a young man, the way I had done, but to me, everything had changed when we had decided to get married. I guess growing up with parents who are unfaithful can make one hypersensitive and it becomes the last thing on earth one wants to experience. The truth is, before I married Robert, I was unfaithful myself and played around a lot, breaking hearts. I was learning that what you do to others you will get back a thousand times.

Another time, a few years later, he once again told me about another side step, and this time it was with one of my best friends, but at that time, I was more at peace with myself and I wasn't afraid in the way I had been so I handled the situation better. To my relief he also said he never went all the way with either of the women, something that made me feel a little better. But even though I was way more centered in myself and could hear the truth, there was a part of me that still felt betrayed.

I often wondered why I would stay with Robert and not leave him. Why did I attract this in the first place? Was I simply as weak as I thought my mom was, as she was living in an unhealthy relationship? Or did I stay and use my marriage as a way of growing? Since we obviously also had our kids, I wanted it to work out for them as well.

My longing to become more resilient and to evolve more spiritually was often the motivation to stay; was this also one of those situations? The questions were many. I had learned that I was projecting a lot of myself onto him. The sides that I didn't like about myself were the things that I really didn't like about him and the stuff that I was still clinging to from the past were the things that came up over and over.

Of course I also loved Robert very deeply, and still do, more than ever. I didn't want to lose him. We had so many things in common, had experienced so much together, and had grown so much that I just did not want to throw that away.

I wanted to build the perfect family and give our kids a nice stable upbringing—something I never had. Like a mama bear protecting her den and her cubs with her claws, I dug in, even though it was a really hard time for a while. Through this time, I often thought of divorce and doubted that I could sustain the kids and myself, living alone. I wanted to stick to my commitment to get through my doubts and work on releasing the resistance.

I often felt like Robert didn't love me. Sure he was attracted to me, and we had great sex, but I always wanted more: more affection, more understanding, more touching, more encouragement, etc. I never felt like I got what I wanted. He was never enough. The coach told me to let go of all expectations I had around him, and that helped, at least at times when I kept them to myself and didn't say something. He would then experience more freedom to be who he was and feel less pressure from me. But she also taught me that I was responsible for my own happiness and as much as I wanted to point a finger at him and blame him for my misery, there were always 3 fingers pointing back at myself. Sometimes Robert would be feeling very high from releasing his old resistance and then he would shower me with his love, maybe because he felt so much love and gratitude within that it would just pour out in all directions.

The coach and I worked a lot on my emotions, and it helped Robert. As he felt more "support" from me, he also started to play even better. He played really well in 2006, so he qualified for the Ryder Cup Team. I was super excited and really wanted to go to the event.

Both the coach and Robert thought it would be better if I stayed at home and reluctantly, I agreed. I wanted to break through the desire to come, as The Ryder Cup is a huge thing, almost as much for the wives as for the players. Robert's work with the coach was very much built on staying in the present and not getting too caught up in what is going on outside. They had the feeling that I might not be able to stay focused and centered, so I never went. Robert got feedback from one player that it was refreshing that a wife chose to stay at home and not get caught up in all the hype. If he only knew! It was my husband's first Ryder Cup for goodness' sake. And I really wanted to be there, but I stayed at home and really worked hard on releasing whatever it was that was in the way and tried to make the best of the situation. To my delight I got another chance to go, Robert qualified to the following Ryder Cup 2008 and that was a whole lot different. This time I went without expectations and with the idea to be as centered as I could be without being caught up in the hype, fame, results etc. It was an amazing experience and we had a lot of fun.

Very often, I made choices trying to please everybody around me. And in my longing to do the right things, I often compromised with what I actually wanted. That always backlashed, especially towards Robert, since he was the one who knew me best and I could be most honest with him.

He felt more and more often that he didn't know who I was. One moment I was the loving wife, cooking dinner and serving, the next I was furious and could not stand being with him.

I felt within that I wanted more from him. I wanted him for myself. I didn't want to share him with the world. I didn't care about golf and his career. I cared about him as a husband and father of our kids.

There were so many times I made choices that I wanted to make to be a good wife and a highly evolved spiritual being, that could expand beyond my conditioning and set myself free. I pushed myself further and further in my longing to be a free human being, free from my internal slavery. I did break through many times and had huge insights but looking back I can see that by pushing I wasn't completely honest as I didn't stand up for myself and what I actually felt. I was so fearful of Robert cheating on me, I acted out of un-alignment because of the lack of not having what I wanted: a fully committed husband. I chose to be identified with victimhood and not being good enough, which attracted more of that into my life. Today I now know that when I am aligned with my true self, it always feels good, and from that space I attract what I truly want and deserve.

Our wedding was another time when I didn't stand up for myself completely. I had always wanted my wedding to be something special and of course I wanted all my friends to be there and my family. It seemed like it wasn't a big deal for Robert, but to me it was. I wanted it to be my wedding, done in my way, but I really wanted to get married so I compromised. Somewhere within I wanted to have a freer wedding without the old conditioning and traditions. So we worked together with the coach on how we could achieve that. Part of me thought it was a great idea, but at the same time, it was far from what I wanted. I wanted the grand princess wedding in a church with a big party. Instead, we married in Lulea, at a hotel, and had a ceremony in a Sami tipi. It was a very small and intimate wedding, very cozy and beautiful but not what I dreamt of. There were few invites; most of the guests were from the circle of friends that we were working with and a few of our old and close friends. My best friends from childhood were not there and neither were my parents. My parents were invited but decided not to come. They felt neglected. I didn't have a bachelorette party or a honeymoon. But there were things that were very magical and very loving with the wedding.

What I came to learn years later was that there is nothing wrong with wanting anything. What made me regret the event was that I didn't stand up for that. I believed that I had to let go of all my desires to feel really free and happy. Today I know that there is a difference between having a desire that is pure coming from one's inner knowing, and a desire that is coming from a sense of lack or need. For years I felt resentful about this event and hammered on myself feeling guilty. I am now very grateful for how it happened since it was a learning experience, helping me identify my path of least resistance.

Have you ever been in a similar situation? Where you felt betrayed in one way or the other? Did you stay or leave? What was the thing that made you stay? What was the thing that made you decide to leave? If you would have done the opposite to what you did, how do you think that would have changed your life? Looking back, do you regret the choice you made? Could you have done something differently? If so, what could you have done instead? Did you ever feel like the third wheel even though you should feel like the only wheel for your partner? What did you do about it? If you ever felt that you compromised with what you truly desired what did you do? Could you have done something differently? Do you believe that in order to be good and have good life you have to be unselfish? What does it mean to be selfish and unselfish to you? What makes you feel the best? Do you prefer to be right rather than to feel good?

Chapter 18

A NEW HOME

How do geese know when to fly to the sun?
Who tells them the seasons?
How do we humans know when it is time to move on?
As with the migrant birds, so surely with us, there is a
voice within if only we would listen to it, that tells us
certainly when to go forth into the unknown.

—Elisabeth Kubler-Ross

I traveled with the coach many times, and a lot of the times to the USA since she lived both there and in Sweden. Several years earlier she had started a foundation in the USA that she decided to start up again; the foundation was benefitting kids at risk and it was a great concept to teach kids how to take personal leadership in their own lives. As we did that, we ended up renting an apartment together in the Seattle area so that we could start working with the foundation more.

One day when we were out shopping, we stopped by a furniture store. I had a strong feeling I had to go in there to look at this magnificent dinner set. It was a huge rustic oak table with ten huge chairs; the store was elegant and trendy. I said to myself, *I want this table! But I do not need it, and I don't have a place for it.* And I didn't, especially since we were at the time living in Monaco and had all the furniture we needed, and it wouldn't fit it in the Swedish vacation home either. But the feeling was so intense. I kept telling the coach that there was something about that table.

We kept talking about it and what I felt, and since Robert had also had a great year on the course and earned the right to play on the USPGA tour the following year, the idea was born to move fulltime to the USA.

After we had an apartment for a year or so, it became clear that we were going to move to the US fulltime. Robert played most of his golf there, and we felt that Monaco was not the best place for the kids to grow up in either. In April 2010, Robert played at Hilton Head, South Carolina, and the kids had Easter break, so they were with him and a friend of ours at the tournament. I was with the coach in Seattle and over a period of time, we had thrown different ideas around on where to look at a new base. We ended up in the southeast part of the country. Robert gave me some things he wanted us to look for: good airport with international connections, nice climate, and not Florida (he did not like Florida particularly). Robert suggested, "Why don't you go to and have a look at Charlotte? I have played there and know a few people." He also loved it when he was there playing. The coach and I decided to go there and have a look while Robert was playing. After finishing, he came up to join us. Then an incredible thing happened: An Icelandic volcano erupted and spread ash over a great part over the northern hemisphere and hence stopped all flights to Europe for a couple of weeks. To our delight, the kids got an extended holiday.

There was a great sense of being at home in Charlotte. People were extremely friendly and warm. The house that we ended up buying was huge and felt like a castle, at 9000 sq. ft. It had a swimming pool, a guest house/mother-in-law suite, and was located on a beautiful lot next to the 12th hole of a golf course.

The move was quick, and I felt like I had left Monaco in haste. It was a stressful and sad time to leave the life that I loved in Monaco, but at the same time it was exciting to start something new. Moving was challenging, but it felt like it was the best choice for all of us in the family. Still, I was a bit worried. What was I going to do there? I didn't know anybody besides the coach, her daughter, who started working as Robert's assistant, and her daughter's son.

When the kids and I arrived in August 2010, the house felt empty. The house had been empty for almost three years because of the economic recession of 2008. The container with all of our boxes and the furniture from Europe arrived in late September, so the kids had to be inventive and come up with different games since they didn't have any toys yet. It was amazing to see the creativity that blossomed. Out of the boxes that came from the new furniture that we ordered, they made houses and board games, and out of the packaging material they made all kinds of stuff: golf clubs, soccer balls, little people, and animals. We also had an empty lot next to our house, so the kids made huts amongst the trees. It was a time full of bliss, joy, and growth for all of us.

As we were looking for the right school, we decided that the best thing to do was to homeschool. That way the kids and I could travel to see Robert if needed, and the kids could adjust to the new environment and language in a better way. All the three kids went to school together, and we had tutors to come in to teach. The coach and her daughter lived in our guest house in the beginning to help us set up everything, and later they both moved out to their own homes. It was a time full of intense growth, and amazing discoveries as we built up the new home.

Have you ever moved to a new place? How was your experience? What made you move in the first place? Were you "guided" to do so, or were there other factors that "made" you move? Was it a good feeling of letting go of the old and moving into the new? What did you discover about yourself, coming to this new place?

Chapter 19

FEEDING THE RIGHT WOLF

The Tale of Two Wolves

A grandfather is talking with his grandson and he says there are two wolves inside of us, which are always at war with each other. One of them is a good wolf, which represents things like kindness, bravery, and love. The other is a bad wolf, which represents things like greed, hatred, and fear. The grandson stops and thinks about it for a second then he looks up at his grandfather and says, "Grandfather, which one wins?" The grandfather quietly replied, "The one you feed."

D uring this time coming to the US and working very closely with the coach, she stayed with us on and off; I experienced a lot of magic, synchronicity, and growing as a human being. At the same time, something wasn't feeling quite right. I noticed that I had a hard time taking feedback, and I struggled with myself. I often felt like a failure, stopped being spontaneous, and I lost the feeling of freedom. I often felt stuck and like I was never good enough. Maybe this was due to feeling I had to run all my decisions by her to get her opinion since she "knew" better than me. Mainly because she had worked more on her connection to the source and hence had a better understanding of what was the "best choice." Or perhaps it was that she was so good at seeing my resistance, not wanting to let go of certain things. Probably both are true, but either way, after some time it became very hard to have her so close. I felt like I was constantly on alert, and rightly so, since her job was to coach me, and I had asked her to call the truth on me.

Even though I wanted to grow quickly, her constant feedback to me became too intense and too much. Maybe it was true that I wanted to keep holding on to certain illusions, but it wasn't always helpful to be confronted with that over and over. Maybe I wasn't ready to let go, even though parts of me wanted to. One part of me wanted to say yes and move beyond my conditioning and let go of everything that was in the way of becoming more of myself. The other part was resisting. The conflict within made it hard to handle the situation.

I was stuck in what seemed to me like an unsustainable situation, where Robert wanted to work with her and I wanted to stay with Robert, so I suffered silently. I also found that the coach focused on calling the truth on the stuff that to her was holding me back. And sure, that was necessary, especially if you have played a victim as I have done. But the more I resisted the feedback she gave the more I unconsciously attracted it since with my strong emotions surrounding the issues, I sent out enormous amounts of energy that the universe responded to and sent back to me. I can see today how I totally created that experience. But the thing that I think I struggled with the most was that we never moved beyond looking at all the stuff and conditioning that needed to be let go.

She picked up my feelings and felt like she was less welcomed, and she spent less time at our house as a result of that. I felt sad, confused and guilty over that, but at the same time I felt a relief.

I see that often in my life I have been looking for somebody to show me, to guide me, to serve the truth on the platter for me, because I thought that doing the job myself to figure things out would be too difficult, and I didn't think that I had it within me. I think just because I never learned to trust my own gut feeling entirely, I became a follower, believing that I knew less than others. At times that made me feel manipulated. I could never have felt manipulated the way I did if I had not believed that the person knew better than me. I know that people around me have done their best, thinking they were helping me.

The coach did help in many ways. I learned many great things about myself, and maybe the most important thing was that I learned to question the situation and become a more critical thinker. As a coach myself today, I have come to understand that it is important to pay attention to which wolf one is feeding. There are as many roads to Rome as there are ways of coaching people. Today, my job is to assist the client to find what they know is the truth for them and to just hold them accountable to what they know and decide to do. I also know that the only thing we can do is to align oneself with ones own truth. Your truth doesn't necessarily have anything to do with somebody else's truth. There are as many truths as there are people living on this planet, since we all have a different vibration and are on different journeys.

Have you ever experienced that you are feeding a part of yourself that is not leading you forward to happiness but rather keeps you in the shadows of something or somebody? How do you think you can identify what is the best "wolf" to feed? Do you blame others for what you feel or are you taking action to feed the right side of yourself that can lead you forward to happiness? What is your own truth built upon?

Chapter 20

A PASSION FOR MUSIC

Out of the shadows and into the sun
Dreams of the past as the old ways are done
Oh, there is beauty and surely there is pain
But we must endure it to live again
—Bruce Dickinson

A s I grew up with music and sang in the school and church choir, I had developed a great interest in music. But it wasn't jazz that caught my attention, even though it was very soothing, and I had to learn how to live with it since my bedroom was next to my dad's home studio. It might have been inner frustration that made me go from being a roller boogie, dancing queen on roller skates to the rebellious spirit that drew me to heavier rock. My dearest cousin Karolina, who was like a sister to me, had developed an admiration for Sid Vicious and the Sex Pistols, and as I was only 11, that sort of music was kind of scary. But as I poked around in my dad's discotheque, containing about 250,000 records and recordings, I found Deep Purple, and from then on, I developed a deep sense of love for the British rock and heavy metal music. First and foremost came Iron Maiden, but then of course came Judas Priest, Black Sabbath, and Ozzy Osbourne, Rainbow, Saxon, Dio, and many more. My first concert, if you can call it that, was outside The Ice Stadium in Stockholm, and Thin Lizzy performed the Renegade tour, in 1981. Since my cousin Karolina and I couldn't afford to get tickets, being only 13 and 15 years old, we were sitting outside the arena, pretending we were inside. But I got a scarf! Still have it somewhere.

I don't know how much money I spent on concerts, but it was a lot and I loved them. It gave me a sense of getting out of control and throwing myself in with a vengeance. I saw several concerts per year and tried to catch Iron Maiden as often as I could.

When I was in my early twenties working at the Body Shop, I had left much of the Heavy Metal rocker identity, and was more of an R&B girl. I went out one evening at the notorious Café Opera in Stockholm, where the rich and famous would hang out. In the crowd next to the bar, I saw a familiar face and then two. I thought to myself, "S…, it is Iron Maiden!" I couldn't resist going up and talking to them and asking what they were doing in town. Of course, their manager interrupted and told me they were having a concert the next day. How could I have missed that? Well, they had gone through some changes as well and had a new lead singer. It turns out the manager put me on the VIP list, and I went there with my friend: first row. And of course, I loved it and wondered how I could have been so stupid to ever stop listening to them. They told us to come and see them at the Strand Hotel after the concert. I had to go there! These guys were my biggest idols. So I did go, and, since I had an invitation to the Ace of Base release party at the Grand Hotel, just close by, we invited the boys to come with us. And so they did. I was so proud when I entered the posh party with Steve Harris, Nicko McB(r)ain, and Janick Gers, all right by my side. Unfortunately, I lost them while mingling at the party, and maybe they felt a bit lost with the Ace of Base crowd. People always asked if something else happened between us and started calling me a groupie, something that was so far from the truth. In my experience The Maiden boys were extraordinarily polite and actually came off as a bit shy. And I was never interested in them in that kind of way. I was very judgmental of girls who were groupies, most likely because of what I had experienced in my past and having a dad in the business, and I just thought it was nasty behavior.

But hey, I was lucky, and as so many times in my life, destiny comes along and shows me that if you let go, what is truly yours will come back.

In 2008, Robert played the Ryder Cup in Valhalla, Louisville, Kentucky. I found, to my great surprise and delight, that one of the Maiden's members; Nicko McBrain was the special team "mascot" and had two big drum sets set up in our team room. I was thrilled to meet him again, and as I introduced myself told him, "Just so you know we have actually met before." He seemed very uncomfortable and didn't really know where to look. Maybe he was afraid I was going to tell him all kinds of bad stuff that we had done, but he didn't remember. I said, "Don't worry, nothing happened. We were just hanging out." Nicko is the sweetest and is very funny. He taught us all to play a little, and of course he did a performance for us. What a treat! We got to know each other a bit, and since then he has been extremely helpful and kind to try to help us get Iron Maiden tickets a few times so we can come and see him play.

After Robert's and my first unofficial "date," I accidentally missed my flight to New York, where I was going to see my current boyfriend at the time. I overslept due to a late night going to a Metallica concert with my cousin Karolina. Robert had followed along at the last minute, since we had a spare ticket and he came home with us afterward. Robert likes to brag about it since it was very random that I would take him to a heavy metal concert on our first "date". But he knows now that I am and always will be a heavy metal rocker at heart.

During the years we lived and worked in Lapland, I was also a member of a band called: This Band. We did mainly covers, and I was more in the background singing and playing percussion. It was a great time, and we even made a recording and went on a small tour. I had the chance to perform and sing one of my favorite songs ever, "Smoke on the Water," a classic by Deep Purple. My dream was fulfilled! I had also dreamed for a long time of learning how to play the guitar and at least be as good as my brother who also had played in a band. When I was on one of my trips with Robert, we were in Ohio, and I had a strong feeling to go into a Guitar Center. I told Robert I was just going in to look. One hour later I came out. He was, of course, wondering what happened to me. I smiled with a big smile saying, "The cutest Navajo Indian just sold me this." And I pulled out the most beautiful guitar, a rosewood Martin acoustic guitar with a fantastic sound. Robert shook his head as he usually does when I have done something crazy. "And what are you going to do with that and what is the bill?" he asked. "Oh, uh, I'm going to learn how to play the guitar and it wasn't much," I mumbled. "It was on sale." He looked up squinting at me to see if I was telling the truth. "Uh, yes, it was cheap, only a grand!!" Robert just shook his head answering, "Yeah, you are crazy." I don't think he ever expected me to start playing since he was so used to me embarking on projects that I never completed. It was my self-sabotage habit that had been ongoing for too long.

Anyway, one day in Monaco, when Thea was about seven, I had to take her to check her ears at the hospital, and as we were sitting there in the waiting room, I saw a man with long dark hair only in a way too short hospital gown. He was in his 40s, with a weathered and torn face, like he had been living a hard life. He was very grumpy and kept grunting and talking to himself with a complaining and irritated voice. There was something up with him that was very interesting, and I kept on peeking at him not knowing why.

About a month later I was dropping Thea by the ballet and decided to pass one of the Churches in Monaco on my way home, when I collided with a big man with a guitar. It was the man from the hospital. I couldn't stop myself from asking if he was a guitar teacher, and he said yes. His name was Gabriel; he was Argentine and a devoted Catholic. He was also an old musician with a rock and roll past. He became my guitar teacher and taught me to not only play the guitar, but to create some lovely music. He had a fascinating past. He was a very much involved in helping Christians in Bethlehem. As well as being a member of several orders, he also had a history of Knights Templar connections. Something I discovered after I had moved from Monaco and that I had more connection with.

My music career kind of ended when I left Monaco, and my dear guitar, which I so lovingly had named after my grandmother Vera, was given away to Gabriel as a goodbye gift.

I tried to look for a new teacher in the states, but I never found anyone as talented and passionate as Gabriel. I decided to give my fingers some rest and grew my nails out and turned my interest to another form of art, namely ballroom dancing. Playing the guitar is still a passion of mine, and hopefully I will go back to it someday.

Have you ever experienced that you had a feeling to talk to somebody you didn't know who it was, but you decided not to do it? How do you think it would have changed your life if you did approach the person? It's so easy to neglect our inner knowing, brushing it away like it was an annoying fly. Imagine what could happen if we would honor all of those hunches.

Chapter 21

RETURNING TO DANCE

Life isn't about waiting for the storm to pass. It's about learning how to dance in the rain.

—Vivian Greene

I started dancing when I was around five-six years old, but at that time it was mainly moving to the rhythm of music a la the 70s style. When I turned about 8, I started ballet in a retired ballerina's home basement, where a fat guy was playing the piano. I loved it even though my teacher was pretty stern. The teacher had a sister who reminded me of one of the mean sisters in the Cinderella story, maybe because she seemed so judgmental and bitter. She was kind of tall and thin. Her face was pale and stern. She looked weak, like she would break any minute, and she was mean. I danced there for about ten years. When I was twelve, I was told that I had no chance to be a successful dancer since I was too tall. If I wanted to stand a chance, I had to work extremely hard so that I could become a soloist dancer. Truth was, I was just early in my development and tall for my age.

I have wondered if the teacher understood how much that comment affected me? My dream as a dancer died that day, and there was just no meaning in continuing. And why should I, since there was no future for me? I'm still wondering what would have happened if she had encouraged me instead, telling me that if I wanted to pursue my dream, anything was possible?

Would I have had the confidence to become a more successful dancer? I don't know. But I now know that I had my revenge, to put it bluntly. It came almost 30 years later when I would prove her wrong.

One sunny day in Charlotte, in January 2012, it was an unusually warm day. I was going with a dear friend on the greenway and on the way back to the parking; I passed a place that looked like a workout studio. Music was pouring out through the wide open door onto the pavement and street. I felt a warm and welcoming feeling coming through from the interior and was so drawn to the energy coming from the place that I peeked inside. The studio had a beautiful ballroom floor, a mirrored wall, and pictures of dancing couples on the walls. A couple was dancing on the floor, in what looked to me like the waltz. They were swirling around and laughing. As they saw me, they danced all the way up to me and the man struck a pose and showed the lady off. She looked at me smiling and said: "Come on in!" I asked what kind of place this was, and they explained it was a ballroom studio. The guy's name was Max, and he was a blond, happy guy from Russia, and the woman seemed to be at least 20 years older. I was taken by their enthusiasm and joy and thought to myself, *I want this too!* I got a pamphlet with the information from them about the studio and took it home. Shortly after that, I went back to shop for a gift card.

That year for Valentines, I gave five lessons to Robert, as a token of my love and to finally do something together that had nothing to do with golf! As I knew he was probably going to say no, the coach helped out and asked him for me. He hesitated at first, but since we were invited to a wedding that year, he committed to doing the five lessons. I knew that was a big step since he had thought of himself as having no sense of rhythm, expect when it came to golf!!

Our teacher was a handsome young Belarusian guy called Pasha. He was delighted to teach us and was excited to find out that Robert was a pro athlete. At first, it was challenging to dance with Robert as he was so used to gripping the golf club with determination and strength, that he grabbed me in the same way. Our moves were stiff and clumsy at first, and as I am much shorter than him, he stepped on me a lot. But his heart was in the right place and, as he is a stubborn man, wanting to be the best he could be, he made some great improvements. After the five lessons, we were both hooked and continued to take more and more lessons. When Robert went back on tour to compete, I continued practicing.

One day it was time for the Studio's showcase, and my instructor approached me and asked if I wanted to do a number. At first I hesitated, thinking, *Why would anybody want to see me dance? I'm just nobody with very little talent.* But as I looked at the other students, I could see how that could make me become a better dancer, so I decided to give it a try. It was terrifying, and I was so nervous. Pasha and I had performed a poetic number to the famous song: "Je suis malade," by the French songwriter, Serge Lama. It's a beautiful song about being in love and alone. The lyrics were very fitting indeed as I could very much identify with the character. And the version we were dancing to was sung by Lara Fabian, who sings it with so much soul and heart that it penetrates deeply into one's being. In the number, I was wearing a white dress. As I poured my essence into the song and sang the words in my mind, I let go and allowed my body to take over, and the number came out pretty good for a beginner. The audience clapped wildly, and Pasha was so proud of me. Interestingly enough, and to my horror, Robert just left the studio with Thea and Ceasar, our kids, and went home. I became startled and worried and started to wonder if he didn't like it. Or maybe he was even jealous of Pasha and me.

It was not until we got home and I saw the big surprise—that there was a bouquet of flowers on the table, and a big ice bucket with Champagne on the ice waiting for me—that I understood that everything was fine. He finally looked me in the eyes, smiling and saying the words I will never forget, "Congratulations! You did great! That was your first 'Ryder Cup!'"

Wow!! I was shocked. He actually liked it. And in his mind, it was similar to the Ryder Cup: one of most prestigious events in any professional golfer's career! He then continued, "I have never seen you like this. I have never seen you so committed before, so determined to get what you want." As he continued, I could see how touched he was by my performance. I then realized how true it was what he said. My life had been scattered for so long; seeking and seeking for the thing that would make me happy and starting new endeavors and projects, never to be able to finish them off, either because I became overwhelmed or too bored. It was a great way of self-sabotaging and playing the victim. I realized how frustrating it had been for Robert, who so easily could focus on one thing at a time, hence his great success as a professional golfer. He was indeed an inspiration in my life. I had learned from him that to be successful, you have to be in the moment, focusing on one thing at a time. He was happy that I had proved to myself and to him that I could indeed change and focus differently. I had started to get in touch with my true powers, and it gave him a taste of what was about to come and of who I truly was. From that day on, he supported me totally and encouraged me to take more lessons and to pursue my newfound passion.

Both of us started taking individual lessons separate from each other. Robert had two amazing female coaches: Nataly and Karolina. Beautiful and lovely young ladies, they taught him how to move like he never had before; it was hilarious at first, but as he is such a determined person, he became a decent dancer. He also competed, something I never thought would happen, but it was a chance for him to do something so completely different from his golf. I improved myself more and more, and one day, my teacher Pasha proposed that I should compete in a competition in Atlanta. I hesitated at first since I historically really dislike competitions overall, and it scared me. But my fear couldn't stop me because I liked the idea of growing, so I decided to do it. It was an amazing experience, and for the first time, I truly understood what Robert was going through all those years as a professional athlete. I ended up doing really well, and I got more taste for competing. Competing in the ballroom category as an amateur is an orgy of sorts. If you have the money you can buy yourself beautiful dresses. And they are not cheap: anywhere between from $1000 to $10,000. Then there is the professional makeup and hairdos every time it's time to compete or do a show. Luckily, I had some experience in doing makeup myself that came in handy when needed. Starting to compete in ballroom was really not what I had planned, as I am not the typical person who likes extravagant dresses, but rather keeps a low profile when it comes to clothing. When Pasha helped me to buy my first ballroom dress, I was freaking out. I didn't really want to wear something that stood out. I wanted something neutral. As I tried to steer him toward elegant, but low key dresses, he kept turning his head. Instead he pulled out a strong colored, aqua dress for my standard ballroom and what to me looked like a circus outfit with rainbow colors, for my Latin dancing. *What? I can't do this! This is way too much extravaganza, and way too scary for me*, I thought. But as I put the dresses on, he smiled and said I looked beautiful. I looked at myself in the mirror. And what I saw was a beautiful woman, who couldn't help smiling. It looked beautiful on. This was my dress. I surrendered and started owning the idea that colors were my thing.

The dresses resonated with my being, and Pasha knew that I needed to step into being visual, in order to be able to step up to the plate and be the best dancer I could be.

Ballroom dancing was not only a great exercise, it was life changing for me and helped me heal, explore, and expose my femininity, and I was forced to do it on the dance floor. It taught me how to trust men again, allowing them to lead me forward without giving up my own sovereignty and daring to overcome all assaults from the past, and what they had done to me. Now I worked on becoming the true beautiful woman I was. It was a lot thanks to the dance and Pasha, who always respected me with his gentlemanly manners, which made it possible. I found that, by allowing myself to express more of all the parts of me that I had covered up so long—my sexuality, sensuality, my power and wildness—I became more whole as a woman. And for every step I took, I allowed myself to let go more and more of the old beliefs that I had been holding on to.

Have you ever danced like nobody's watching? And have you ever tried just to let your body move and see what happens if you allow it to guide you? If you have not, I urge you to try it and see what kind of emotions come up for you. The body will never lie. I strongly encourage you to start dancing, especially ballroom, since it's such an amazing journey into oneself. I have seen men and women overcoming fear and becoming more of themselves through dancing and I hope one day dancing will be part of the curriculum in school since it heals, it teaches us about body awareness and awareness about ourselves, as well as our connection with others. If you haven't seen the movie "Dancing in Jaffa" I recommend you watch it. Dancing can heal people and the planet.

Chapter 22

THE VOICE WITHIN AND PRUNING THE BUSHES

Stop looking for the answers from strangers. The answers to your life are within you. Only you know what makes your heart feel at home. Only you can hear your inner voice. The key is in asking the right questions.

—C. Nordyke

The fall of 2012 was a transformative time. Starting to dance had helped me come out of my shell and unleashed my powers in a whole new way. I discovered how much I had been holding myself back. I could not hide from what my body was telling me, and

I thrived on exploring my emotions, but I was still struggling with my life: as wife to Robert, as a mom, and with the coach.

One night in November, I awoke with a great sense of urgency; a voice inside of me said, *You have to set the tenth alignment!* It was like a calling from my soul, a silent but determined urge coming from somewhere inside of me. I had no clue to what it meant, and I started to call my mom to ask her if it was something astrological that was going on. (We didn't think about it at the time, but it was something going on; about a year later, I figured out that the whole consciousness on the planet was shifting.) She said she didn't know, so I started to search on Google. After a lot of searching, I finally found something that caught my attention. It was a blog by Christine Hoeflich, and she talked about listening within and connecting to your higher self. From her book, *What Everyone Believed: A Memoir of Intuition and Awakening*, she writes:

> *And contrary to what you may have been led to believe, the "separation" from your higher self was something your higher self actually engineered, for some highly noble purposes, too: for the learning experiences that would benefit not only you, but your family, your community, and the rest of humanity.*

Even though I had supposedly worked with communicating with my higher self before, to me this was a new level where not only my mind was involved, but also my body and my emotions. I got her book and downloaded her program and started practicing the exercises. It gave me practical exercises on how to reconnect the heart with the mind through the higher heart, the connection to source/God.

It became evident that I had to change something. A friend of mine had gone through some changes in her business and had read the book

Necessary Endings by Dr. Henry Cloud. She recommended that I read it, and it was so timely. I had, for a long time, identified myself, and my journey of growth, with the rose. My heart resonated deeply with the analogy: about being a gardener and pruning, as he so wisely puts it in his book. Dr. Henry assisted me greatly in seeing more clearly what I needed to do.

> *Determine whether "pruning" is necessary for growth.*
>
> *In order for a rose bush to achieve its full growth potential, every good gardener knows that it must be carefully pruned. There are three circumstances in which a gardener prunes a rose bush: 1) when the bush produces more buds than it can sustain, 2) in order to remove parts of the bush that are diseased, and 3) to remove dead branches in order to make way for new growth.*
>
> *First, when the bush produces more buds than it can sustain, the overgrowth drains essential resources from the bush, and the gardener must choose which of the "good" buds are "best." He then prunes the good buds so that all of the bush's resources can be focused on helping the best buds thrive.*
>
> *Our lives and businesses are just like the rose bush. We may have a lot of excellent strategies, products, activities, relationships, or ideas that we've poured our resources into. But if we pruned some of the good stuff back, we would enable the best parts to get all that they need to thrive, making our businesses and relationships even more productive and happier.*
>
> *Second, when parts of the rose bush are diseased, and every effort to nurse them back to health has failed, a gardener must prune the diseased parts to prevent them from spreading. Similarly, in business, when all of the coaching, mentoring and training you've offered cannot make some employees more productive, or a strategy you've worked on isn't producing the results you'd hoped*

for, it's time to get out the pruning shears. Whether products or people, there are some elements of our business and personal lives that cannot be helped and letting them go—whether temporarily or permanently—is essential to your survival.

Third, many branches are already dead, and taking up space that living branches need in order to grow. Similarly, there are many aspects of business that have run their course and can no longer contribute to the company's success. Those parts of the business must be shut down so that the rest of it can thrive. And in our personal lives, there are many activities and people that aren't conducive to our health or growth, and must be lovingly pruned.

That's quite a paradox: letting go is the way to grow. Make space for the new. Prune! Well, I knew I had some pruning to do, and it scared me. It was time to change things up. I needed to be more present, less bound by habit and routine, and not so reliant on the opinions of others. I decided to stop working with the coach.

It was terrifying. First of all, she was a close friend, but secondly, she was working with Robert. And by ending my working relationship with her, I thought that I risked losing Robert and the kids as well. But I had to do it. I could no longer live the way I was. It was time to offload what *had* served me and upload what *would* serve me.

When I finally told the coach in an email in November 2012, I felt a tremendous relief. I went back to meditating again after so many years thinking I didn't need it, and started building my inner communication from scratch, something that was hard since there was a lot of conditioning that needed, you guessed it, pruning! I felt like I had been following a path that was not mine. It was time to change the direction and start building my own bridges. Even though I had started the journey of listening within years before, I had also come to doubt myself and what I felt, because of so many times relying on other people's opinions, making their opinions more important, and thinking that they knew better.

As I continued to practice this new way of connecting within and beyond my mind and trusting my body more and relying on what I was feeling, I also started becoming aware of the myriads of little symbols that were coming my way. It could be a number that constantly reappeared or a person who recommended a book or a website, or some creature from the animal kingdom. I noticed that I was so much more connected to the all, the greater picture, the one. I recognized that everybody in my path had something important to give; that everybody was my teacher and guide. It was like waking up from having been living in a bubble that had become too tight to live within.

And as I went back to the old knowledge I had gained earlier in my life but forgotten about, I started to become aware of all the little messengers from life/source/God, that were showing them to me. So many animals, bugs, and birds appeared just when I needed their message. I realized what I have known my whole life: that there is so much old wisdom being made available to us, if we are open to interpreting the magic of their messages. The native people on the planet knew it and were one with Gaia, our beloved home. I started using that old knowledge and interpreted the messages, the animal medicine.

For example, for a long time I had a red cardinal desperately trying to get my attention. He sat on the branch outside my bathroom window and repeatedly flew into the window over and over, almost breaking his poor little head. My logical mind told me he saw his reflection and wanted to scare away this opponent. But something else told me to look it up, and I researched to figure out what he wanted to "say." I found this: The cardinal reminds us to hold ourselves with pride, not ego—pride. The cardinal asks us to stand a little taller, be a bit more regal, and step into our natural confidence, owning that we were born to lead with grace and nobility. According to the site: www.whats-your-sign.com, those who attract the cardinal as their totem are naturally energetic, love life, and happily help others when they can.

Many other animals came to my attention, as I needed to be reminded of those parts within myself: deer, hawks, squirrels, frogs, and the famous cicada that taught me that now was the time to find my voice and speak up.

I was discovering the wonder of living in a world that was always ready to show me something, to help and teach me. Life and I were in an interactive, alive relationship. Far from only affection, we were talking!

Have you ever experienced anything similar? Where many symbols in the world around you are trying to communicate with you? What was it like? And what did you learn?

Chapter 23

AN ANCIENT CONNECTION

The awakening is the purpose. The awakening of the fact that in essence we are light, we are love. Each cell of our body, each cell and molecule of everything. The power source that runs all life is light. So to awaken to that knowledge, and to desire to operate in that realm, and to believe that it is possible, are all factors that will put you there.

—**Dolores Cannon**, *The Convoluted Universe—Book One*

As the cardinal had helped me to step up and be visual, so too, dancing served me, spoke to me, and taught me about my life. And here I learned that all things, even pain and injury, can be a guidepost onto the next perfect path in my life.

As I continued dancing and competing, I developed some problems with my feet and knee, and I looked for a reflexologist to help me out.

I started to Google and found a lady—a reflexologist who also worked with dance sport. I was delighted and booked an appointment. When I met the lady called Anne, it was like a reconnection with an old friend. We had so much in common, and we shared a lot of spiritual beliefs and connections. I had so many questions. My curiosity was hungry since I had put my spiritual seeking on the shelf for over ten years. Besides being a reflexologist, Anne was a Quantum Healing Hypnotist as well, the healing method developed by Dolores Cannon. Dolores was a hypnotist that helped people dealing with habits such as weight loss and smoking; she discovered that clients started to talk about previous lives, and that she could regress the client to heal themselves through healing the previous past lives. Dolores Cannon has written 19 books based on the insights, knowledge, and information she had collected throughout her 45-year career as a hypnotherapist using her Quantum Healing Hypnosis Technique® (QHHT®) to investigate reincarnation and mysteries through past life regression. You can find more info on www.dolorescannon.com.

I had long been intrigued by and interested in the concept of past lives. Here was a chance to find out and experience more! I booked a session with Anne. We met up at her practice, and I lay down on her massage table as she used her soothing voice to put me in the trancelike state. I had no expectations whatsoever, but the stuff I started speaking about was mind-blowing. It was like it was me speaking, but I was listening almost like it was someone else. Each word and idea surprised me, and then I quickly felt like I recognized every thought and picture in my mind.

I suddenly found myself embodied as some kind of extraterrestrial being, living on another a planet. She asked me if I knew the name of the race and the only thing I could say was "Arthurian." It all seemed like a dream and fantasy, but the words just came out of my mouth. Anne asked if I meant *Arcturian*? I answered that I didn't know, but maybe. There were many other things I shared with her, and by the time I got back home and started to listen to the recording, it was fascinating. I had no clue what the Arcturians were and began to Google it. It turned out there was actually a lot of information about them. And there was an extraterrestrial race called Arcturians from the solar system around the star, Arcturus! Go figure! I was shocked and fascinated at the same time. During the hypnosis, I had experienced coming down to this planet to do a job, like a volunteer, to help with the transformation of the earth. I had in my youth always felt that I had some special purpose. But I didn't know what it was. And I had always had an interest in UFOs. I used to look at those kinds of books in my grandfather's library in Spain. Once I had even had a very strong dream where a spaceship landed outside my room at my parents' house. Was I just having a really wild imagination or was there some truth in all this? I started doing some research about the Arcturians and connected with a girl called Frankey. She was English and didn't live far away from me. She was an empath, connecting psychically to the feelings and emotions of others. She did soul readings, so I connected with her to find out more about my exact origin and some sense of my destiny's direction. At the same time I found Suzanne Lie, an author who has been channeling the Arcturians for some time. She has written several books about them and their message. They were sharing that we are multidimensional beings, and the planet was going through big changes of transformation. I learned a lot about multidimensional leadership: how we can act out of a higher version of ourselves and connect with the higher dimensions that the Arcturians come from, the 5th dimension and beyond. I learned that they soon would be showing themselves, but it was very hard for them to be seen in a 3rd-dimensional reality since it is so dense. That explained to me why some people could see UFOs and some not. Could it be that one has to enter a higher state of awareness to be able to see them at all? We had just left 2012 behind. 2012 was a year that had been scary for many people studying the ancient cultures and religions. According to the Mayan calendar, the time as we know it had stopped. Some people interpreted that there was going to be the big Armageddon. (Remember the movie *2012*?) But others that had studied this concluded that we were only transforming into higher energies; as the planet evolved, so did we. One of the most fascinating authors about the secrets of time and hidden knowledge is David Wilcock, whom some of you might know from the TV series on History Channel, *Ancient Aliens*. He has his own shows now: *Wisdom Teachings* and *Cosmic Disclosure* on www.gaia.com, a spiritual online TV station. He is the author of several books that I warmly recommend.

At the same time as I discovered this, my intuition developed even more and as I worked more on meditation, I also started to go back to study the chakras—the energy centers of the body—and how to clear them. I discovered there are many techniques like toning: how one can use the vibration of the voice to balance and heal the body. Toning is an ancient technique that has been used in Mantras and in prayers all over the world.

Have you ever had memories set in a location that you have no memory of visiting? Did you ever have dreams that seemed very real? They could be memories from your past life. I suggest that you can discover more of who you are by paying attention to your dreams and your intuition. There is so much more to discover and understand that we can find by honoring ourselves all the way.

Chapter 24

EVERYTHING IS CONNECTED

I have always quested and still do for the Holy Grail, but I stopped looking in the earthen caves and in the stars. I started questing through the valleys and mountains of my own soul.
—David Paul Kirkpatrick

As I increased my awareness of life reaching out to me with love and information, and as I further opened my consciousness in working with gifted healers and shamans, I started remembering things from before I met Robert, like when I was reading the book, *The Sword in the Stone,* by Terence Hanbury White. It's the legendary story about the boy Wart and the mystical wizard Merlin. The Grail mysteries always had evoked something within me. I dusted off my old tarot card deck and started doing readings again. I realized that a lot of information I had received lately was connected to King Arthur and the ancient legend of the Grail. It was a story that had followed me since childhood. One interesting thing was that the name, Arthur, is derived from the Celtic elements *artos*, meaning "bear," combined with either *viros*, meaning "man," or *rigos*, meaning "king." And supposedly he was an Arcturian. Maybe even more interesting is that the name of the Star Arcturus is derived from ancient Greek Arctouros meaning The Guardian of the Bear. The Greek name is a reference to its being the brightest star in the constellation next to Ursa Major, The Greater Bear. I couldn't help wonder how this was connected to my name and me.

In 1992, I had traveled to Glastonbury with a group from Sweden, guided by our tarot master and astrologer Thomas Jönsson, to learn more in depth about the legend and its mystery. In summary, the legend is this: Joseph of Arimathea was a rich man and a relative of Jesus (and one of his covert disciples), who claimed the crucified body of Jesus from Pilate. He came to Britain with other disciples and founded the first British church at Glastonbury, where he planted his staff. This miraculously flowered into a tree, The Glastonbury Thorn, whose offshoots may still be seen today, flowering every Christmas. Joseph also brought and kept there certain sacred relics, perhaps the Chalice Cup or Grail. He knew Britain from his trips as a tin merchant, and in fact, on one of his trips he had brought his nephew, the boy Jesus. Joseph, and some say the Virgin Mary, is said to be buried there, along with the Grail featured in legends of Arthur—whose official tomb is still to be seen there.

As I walked around there, connecting to its surroundings, the Tor, the Chalice Well, etc., something must have been awakening within me that had been slumbering. Later on the trip, I was fortunate to meet a man there called Palden Jenkins. He, along with Phyllis V. Schlemmer, had been compiling a book called *The Only Planet of*

Choice. It's a book that represents the outcome of a distinguished international research group who has communicated with an enlightened circle of celestial beings known as "The Nine Principals of the Universe" through Phyllis, who was a world-renowned medium and psychic. The source states that, while other planets do have a choice, the consciousness is collective. Only on earth can a soul experience individual choice. Could that be right? That planet earth was the only planet in the universe that had that? Would that mean the reason for so many things being expressed in this reality? Good and bad? Dark versus light? Where one as a soul, being a part of the bigger picture, could experience individuality? Like the drop of water realizing it is a drop and can be separated from the ocean?

Since its launch in 1993, it's been considered as one of the most significant books of our time, and I agree. But at the time it came out, I was only in my early 20s. It was a massive inspiration for me, but I was simply not grounded enough to experience the newer frequencies and profound message of the book. I had a long way to go to be able to comprehend the book and its actual importance.

Anne and I had several QHHT sessions where more memories seemed to appear, and later, when I would be sitting in deep meditation, symbols and messages started to pop up. I started drawing and taking notes. There seemed to be so much more to discover about my past and where I came from. Or was there? Maybe I was just picking up on something? Things started to get more and more interesting. Some of the visions I had in the trance-like state were definitively from another time. Sometimes that looked like the Middle Ages, with castles and me being a knight or a Templar trying to save the Grail. Were these memories from a previous lifetime or perhaps from another dimension? Interestingly enough, my brother Eric had traveled to Malta and discovered a book by coincidence in an antique shop, with Templars' names and crests in it. He had found my mother's maiden name there. Could it be that we had a Templar bloodline? It was also fascinating that I had been unwittingly moving about in secretly significant places I had visited with Robert on his golf tournaments before the kids were born. We liked to visit places outside of the golf tournaments, and one of these sites was Cintra, in Portugal. A place I know now has a lot of secrets and hidden Templar knowledge. As I did more and more research online, I found out that there are many solar systems and many different alien races. Many of the people on Earth have reincarnated from another solar system.

My life experiences started to make more sense as I found a red thread through my wide experiences: the places I had visited and the people I had met. I found that there were many people like me waking up differently from each other, but having the same kind of experiences. It seemed that the whole planet was in a state of awakening.

Have you ever experienced something similar? Do you think it could be possible that we all could be coming from other stars and solar systems? Have you ever experienced going to a place and feeling like you have been there before?

Chapter 25

THE INCA CONNECTION

*Your emperor may be a great prince; I do not doubt it, seeing that
he has sent his subjects so far across the waters; and I am willing
to treat him as a brother. As for your pope of whom you speak, he
must be mad to speak of giving away countries that do not belong
to him. As for my faith, I will not change it. Your own God, as you
tell me, was put to death by the very men He created. But my God
still looks down on His children.*

—**Atahualpa,** Inca Chief (On hearing Pope Alexander VI
had declared Peru to be a possession of Spain)

I n 2013, I found out more about what the tenth alignment meant,
and it had to do with something that an old part of me related to.
As a child, I was very interested in the Native American people

and their culture, and was especially drawn to the Incas (*Incas*, meaning the children of the sun) in Peru. And when I found and started reading the comic series *Tintin*, by the Belgian cartoonist Hergé, I was drawn especially to two of the volumes, interestingly enough: #13, *The Seven Crystal Balls*, and later #14, *The Prisoners of the Sun*, which were both made into animated movies the year I was born, 1969. I loved mysteries and created my own detective club spying on my neighbors. Not so popular, and pretty embarrassing when they discovered what I was trying to do. When I was 18 and had finished *gymnasiet*, I thought about going to Peru to study Spanish but chickened out since I didn't want to go to a school run by a monastery. Also there was hyperinflation and bankruptcy that rocked Peru. The country sought assistance from the International Monetary Fund. Also the guerrillas' bombing and assassination campaign intensified, so I decided to go down another route and studied instead in Murcia, Spain.

My big Spanish project was to write about the Incas. I dreamed about one day going there, which eventually I did. I had a Peruvian friend in Sweden who I met when I worked in a New Age book and crystal store; he recommended that I go and stay with his friend in Lima. He was not there himself, but was generously allowing us to stay in his house. I had expected to go to all the places that I've dreamed of going to: Machu Pichu, Lake Titicaca, Cusco, and Nazca, but as I travelled with the coach and as our intention at that time was to break through all the wants, needings, and longings, we decided to stay put in Lima. Maybe I had too much desire to go. Perhaps there was a great possibility to break through and collapse timelines? And with that I meant to let go of the things one thinks one wants, to undress the desire. Running after desires and thinking that getting something from the outside can make you happy is a temporary thing that will just deal with the urge for a short time. It won't last forever. So the more one chose to let go of the desire, the more internal freedom and joy would arise from the inside. This is much of what the Buddha talked about, letting go of the desire. In retrospect, I think that's what it was. And we had a lot of fun, but a part of me is still regretting not going to see the sacred sites. There was a longing to go there to maybe reawaken something old or heal something. But maybe it was too early or even unnecessary. Who knows?

Instead of going, we watched several movies about all kinds of things. Talk about breaking patterns of the seeker! It was not until the last couple of days, when I probably had let go of all wants and expectations, that I decided to see a Shaman and to try Trichocereus Pachanoi, aka San Pedro, a columnar cactus, native to the Andean mountains of Peru, and Ecuador. It is one of the four most sacred plants of Peru, along with Tobacco, Ayahuasca, and Coca. San Pedro has hallucinogenic properties and is often compared to the more popular cactus known as Peyote; both are members of the mescaline family. Shamans and natives have used San Pedro for at least 3000 years. San Pedro got its name because, in mythology, God hid the keys to heaven in a secret place, and the Christian Saint who was named San Pedro used the powers of the cactus to uncover the secret hiding places of the keys. The cactus was later named after him. Drinking San Pedro brew was a very interesting experience. I drank the tea prepared by the shaman and noticed that even though I had taken my chewing gum out of my mouth just before drinking the concoction, it felt like I was still chewing on it. Very symbolic, considering everything that we experience in the now is actually already an old story, and that what we think and feel today will create and manifest perfectly in the future—The Law of Attraction in essence. I then saw the room dissolving into a rainbow-colored net of frequencies and everything melted together. There were simply no boundaries. That night was horrible as I met my demons and I was terrified. I couldn't sleep the whole night, and I understood that I still had a lot of stuff to let go of.

I have since learned that it is not necessary to grow and evolve by taking psychedelics, but it can increase the process and is an exciting experience if one wants to have a taste of the reality we are really living in. It is also critical, in my opinion, to have an authentic shaman present during the ritual since a lot can happen. The shaman is just not an ordinary person; it's a person who travels in other dimensions, who has the wisdom, and knows how to deal with energy. I know now that it is possible to see different dimensions when taking psychedelics but it is not necessary. Some can see them without psychedelics, too, and experience that they actually do exist. And it is also possible to be too open, so that one leaves one's body and surrenders one's sovereignty, which makes the body vulnerable and open for any other energetic entity to come along and try to attach to you. That almost happened once when I participated in a healing Ayahuasca ceremony, the other sacred plant brew, for the first time in sacred ritual. The word means "the rope of the soul" in the Quechua language. Ayahuasca contains the hallucinogen DMT, Dimethyltryptamine, which is a tryptamine molecule that occurs in many plants and animals. It can be consumed as a powerful psychedelic drug and has historically been prepared by various cultures for ritual and healing purposes. It is also called the "spirit molecule."

I had not done the necessary preparations needed before the ritual since it all came together kind of suddenly. La Dieta is the preparation you do a few weeks before to clean and detox the body. And maybe because I didn't do that, my experience came out pretty rough. Who knows? It was an extremely strong experience, however. Aya, the spirit of Ayahuasca, formed like a demanding snake and carried me on her magical journey. I found myself dissolving and being sucked up by the earth and all kinds of spirits, and entities from the 4th dimension started to appear. Suddenly the energies around me noticed that I was there, open and available, and they were trying to get me. One disturbing entity, in particular, tried to be aggressive and physically familiar with me. Afterwards, I have wondered if it was only a memory from the past that needed to be healed or if it had actually been happening. Whatever it was, I didn't want to surrender to it and fought to the end.

But after the spiritual war was over, the exquisite rise of the Kundalini energy started to linger from the root of my spine and surged, exploding with beauty and power in my heart. It was so amazingly powerful, and it awoke so much more power within me. Today I know that when we are aligned with our true and higher self, we know what we want to do, what we desire is aligned with our highest purpose. When we are unaligned, we often feel lost and empty and we reach for things outside of ourselves, be it an experience, money, or love to fill our emptiness. Therefore it's important to know why we want certain things, and to understand what we think we will achieve by getting what we desire and to know how it will make us feel. Getting into the feeling good state is the key.

Have you identified your desires? What do you think you will gain by getting your desires fulfilled? Did you ever decide to let go of a desire? What happened and what was the outcome? What did you learn? Do you know the difference between a desire that is made out of conditioning and a desire that is aligned with your higher purpose?

Have you ever taken any sacred herbs/ plants? What was your experience? Would you do it again? Why? How do you think it could help you?

Chapter 26

THE TENTH ALIGNMENT

We are stars wrapped in skin. The light you are seeking has always been within.

—Anonymous

K nowing that I had some story with Peru, the Incas, and the Aymara Indians, it maybe wasn't so weird what I came to discover. The meaning of setting the tenth alignment, the words that I had heard inside of me that morning of 2012, was also about connecting to the inner Sun within us and about activating the tenth solar disk. It turned out that the Incas and their successors have been preparing for a great awakening of this planet, and it was about several disks being activated within our bodies as part of this process over what seemed like two decades. As I searched online, I found a lot of information about it. Here is some from the website www.labyrinthina.com:

Peru is a land steeped in ancient prophecies and wisdom that is vital for our planet during these transitional times. Life in the Incan empire was measured by a thousand-year cosmic cycle called an Inti, which means 'Sun.' This thousand-year cycle was then divided into halves, each of which was referred to as a Pachakuti. The cosmovision of the Andean world is the conception of duality that is in permanent opposition, but complementary, like the principle of yin/yang that expresses this opposition between day/night, light/dark, man/woman, earth/sky, up/down. This same principle of duality applies to each Pachakuti. However, Pachakuti also is used to refer to the transitional time that divided each Pachakuti and this is characterized as a time of great changes.

During the five hundred years of the eighth Pachakuti, Pachacuteq, the greatest spiritual leader of the Incas, ruled. This was a time of light when the Inca Empire flourished and there was expansion and good fortune. The ninth Pachakuti, on the opposite side of the duality, brought with it the five hundred years of darkness when the Spanish invaders conquered the Inca and the Indian people lost their power.

We are now entering the tenth Pachakuti, which the local people refer to as the returning of Pachkuteq, the returning of the Light. This is the time when the etheric crystal cities of the fourth dimension—such as the lost golden city of Paititi, Machu Picchu, and the eternal etheric city under Lake Titicaca—will again be available to us.

There is a legend that says at the time Lemuria was sinking, one of the seven Great Masters of Lemuria, Lord Aramu Meru, was given the mission to bring the 12 sacred Golden Solar Discs from the Temple of Illumination to Lake Titicaca for safe keeping. During the time of the Incas, the Solar Disc was transferred to Cusco and placed in the Koricancha, the main temple of the Incas, where it stayed until the coming of the Spanish. At that time, it was returned to Lake Titicaca and placed in the Eternal Etheric City inside the Lake.

In the legend of their origin, this is the place from where the first Incas, Manco Kapaq and Mama Ocalla, entered the Earth. The Solar Disc was used in the capacity of a cosmic computer that received light information directly from the Universal Mind Source, Viracocha, at the center of the galaxy. By entering the Temple of Illumination and opening themselves, the Lemurians, and later the Incas, could access the sacred wisdom. It is during this time, the Age of Pachakuti, that the sacred Solar Disc is to be re-activated, accessing the cosmic wisdom.

As I read and understood, I found that it was the time to catch up and activate the tenth disk, and I continued reading to understand more about it on the website: etonearth.blogspot.com:

Activation of the tenth solar disk

This tenth solar disk that we will activate through the code solar matrix alignment will take us to the soul star chakra and we're synchronized with the planetary Christ Grid through activation of 144 points of light in our brain neural network.

That in turn, will be synchronized to the 144 points of light in their DNA, which were activated with the ninth solar disk.

This will allow their bodies, chakra, and DNA to be synchronized with Christ Grid staff and turn on the planetary Christ Grid.

The Christ Grid personal and the planetary is a spherical shaped tissue, composed by 144 pentagons joined together by points of light.

These two grids and alignment remain in sync with the neural pathways in your brain and there, around the brain like tissue that connects and unifies this consciousness with the Christ consciousness planetary and solar.

In sacred geometry, the planetary Christ Grid and staff relate to the dodecahedron, the twelve-sided polyhedron that is part of the Platonic solids.

Well, the Christ Grid is similar to the dodecahedron, however has 144 sides or pentagons.

Slowly their bodies, minds, and DNA have been expanding and will do even more!

Their bodies are ready! Since solar discs that were activating during the past nine months have enabled light receptacles in each of your chakras, they also have pushed their cells to resonate at a frequency higher octave.

It all seemed like a fairy tale. What did it mean? What was the connection between the numbers and the ancient traditions? There were too many coincidences. I had to take a deeper look, and it resonated in my heart. It would have been good to have some kind of guide to help me understand more about it all, but now I was on my own and had to trust the information that came from inside of me. I was on my way to discover that there was much more to life than I had ever understood. I was a part of a great adventure, and even if I wasn't in Peru, something was taking place within me and on the planet, and it had to do with raising one's energy frequency, by activating the solar power within.

Have you ever wondered about where all the legends come from? Did you know that there are many stories in our ancient culture that all seem very connected? And that many of the stories in the bible, for instance, can be traced to ancient cultures like the Sumerians, and their stories actually influenced the content of the bible. Do you think there could be a connection?

Chapter 27

NUMBERS

*The harmony of the world is made manifest in Form and Number,
and the heart and soul and all the poetry of Natural Philosophy are
embodied in the concept of mathematical beauty.*
—D'Arcy Wentworth Thompson

T he work with Anne was beneficial in reconnecting and opening up to the inner wisdom. One day, I was watching a YouTube clip and felt a connection to a guy interviewed on the show. I told her that we should invite him to come and visit Charlotte. We had both felt for a while that something needed to be done, but we didn't really know what it was until we met Joe. Joe calls himself a spiritual rainbow warrior, and he works with crystals to heal and restore people and the planet. We decided to do a group and see if anybody would be interested in coming. It was the fall of 2015, a time when a lot of things were happening in the world around us.

We had great success with the group and learned a lot about these specific crystals. Joe left behind a book about these crystals, called Vogel Crystals, after the founder Marcel Vogel. I was strongly attracted to them. I found out that I could get my own crystals in a small shop in Asheville: The Points of Light.

I went there and left with two huge, way too expensive Vogel Crystals. I didn't even want to tell Robert. I thought he would blow a fuse, but for me they were necessary to get. I still didn't know why or for what purpose, but as so many times before, I just listened to that voice within that tells me what to do, and the answer usually unfolds after a while. I asked the shopkeepers if they knew anybody who taught how to use the crystals, and they recommended the Vesica Institute for Holistic Studies, an educational center close by the store.

While back home, I looked at the beautiful and impressive pieces. One was hand cut in 13 sides, and the other was 144 sided and machine cut, but both of them were real Vogel Crystals. Marcel Vogel, the founder, was a fascinating figure. He was an intuitive, for sure, and a remarkable man that studied luminescence, the light that can emit from a cold body, like a crystal. Later in life, he started to work for IBM and had around 24 patents. As he discovered the properties of the crystals, he also discovered their healing properties and combining that with sacred geometry turned out to be a success. He even cured himself of a heart attack while driving his car. See Chapter 4 of *The Crystal Wisdom of Marcel Vogel* (www.satyacenter.com). Unfortunately, as far as I know his methods were never published, and he was never well renowned for his excellent studies. He passed away in 1991, and it wasn't until later that his opus was recovered and shared online by his family.

Thanks to Joe and his visit, I immediately connected to The Vesica Institute and felt guided from within to apply to their online course and a live event coming up. It turned out to be a wise choice.

About six months later, I still had not discovered how I should use the Vogel crystals, and I approached a man called the Galactic Historian, Andrew. He was a psychic with abilities to see beyond this solar system and galaxy. Wild enough! I didn't have any experience and was entertained by his stories. I asked him some questions about the crystals, and he told me that one day they would tell me their names, and that the 13 sided one was a crystal that I should keep when I was writing. I thought to myself, *Well then, I'm probably never going to use it.* I did not write much in those days. Little did I know what was going to come. The other one, the 144 sided one, was a power tool, and I knew it from the start as it had felt like a laser gun in my hand. He told me what I could do to get ready to use it, and I listened carefully. Maybe a month or so later I quietly asked the 144 sided crystal what it wanted to be called. Wow and behold, it answered back to me: *Yes, my name is George.* What? That's a funny name for a crystal, I thought. I kind of expected it to be more exhilarating and alien-like, like a formula of some sort. But George? Really?

Andrew had also told me how to treat the crystals as they are living beings. I know it might sound weird, but they can store and transmit energy and information, hence the reason why they are in computers. George didn't really talk much more until I had a Skype call with my rainbow warrior friend Joe. He called to check how it was going and if I had started to work with the crystals yet. No, I answered and then I said, "But he told me his name. It is George!" I think I expected him to start laughing. Instead, he said, "Wow! That's cool, St. George and the dragon!" I started to shiver, and goose bumps came over my whole body, and responded, "What did you just say? Did you say, St. George?" And as I said that I turned my head around and moved away from the screen, so Joe could see what was behind me. The kids had so happily baptized the dining room that I was sitting in as "The Happy Knight's" room when we moved in, because it had a round table, with 12 chairs and a 16th century knight helmet on the table. There was a small icon hanging on the wall. It was the only thing I had left from my grandmother on my mother's side. It was an old Greek icon from probably the 13th century, and an orthodox Christian church, which she picked up on one of her travels going around the world with my granddad. The icon was showing the slaying of a very famous dragon by a very renowned saint: St. George!

When I revisited this text as I was writing this book I learned something more; the crystal named George is also symbolizing the Christ consciousness and 144th grid. And that was what the Incas had talked about. How was this even possible? And why? What was the purpose? Was I supposed to use the "George" crystal as a healing sword? It certainly seemed that way.

I also found some other interesting facts and connections about the number 144.

Number 144 is a blend of the vibrations and attributes of the number 1 and the number 4, the 4 appearing twice and so giving emphasis and extra influence to its energies. The number one symbolizes changes, new beginnings and ventures, ambition and tenacity, self-leadership and assertiveness, uniqueness and individuality, and ambition and will power. It also tells us that we create our own realities with our beliefs, thoughts, and actions. The number four symbolizes the energies of effort and will, building solid foundations, working diligently towards achieving goals, practicality and determination, and honesty and integrity. It also tells of achieving success and reaping the rewards for work well done.

It also reminds us to look to new ways to go about getting your work done more efficiently. Listen to your intuition as your guides are ushering positive energies toward and around you.

It also symbolizes the message to keep your thoughts positive and optimistic as you undertake an important new role or venture. Your positive energies, intentions, and actions will manifest your expected results. Trust that the universe/source/God will deliver all that you'll need.

There was also some very interesting information that I found in The Book of Revelations, in the Bible. Again, in Revelation 14:1ff, John saw the Lamb on Mount Zion. With him were 144,000, sealed with the Father's name upon their foreheads. This great multitude had been "purchased out of the earth," and they were said to be the "first fruits unto God and unto the Lamb." This information could also be found in something called The Emerald Tablets, they both predict and forecast the incarnation and arrival of 144,000 Lightworkers who will save Earth from the "Forces of Darkness" during the *end times.* Most of the 144,000 Lightworkers are now here and in the process of "waking up" to their divine purpose and mission on Earth. The majority of the 144,000 are advanced incarnated Starseeds from more advanced planets, although some of the 144,000 are advanced local souls of Earth. Most of the 144,000 are now in the process of coming out of their long mental and spiritual hibernation, slowly but surely realizing that they are here to assist in the great transformation of Earth. The cellular memories of the 144,000 were programmed, timed, and triggered to "go off" at this time and awaken them to their true identity, mission, and purpose for incarnating on Earth at this most crucial time in Earth's history. The Emerald tablet is said to be a green crystal inscribed with the secrets of the universe. The origin where it was found is unclear but one theory is that it was hidden under a statue of Hermes and clutched in the hands of the corpses of Hermes Trismegistus himself. The name of this figure is derived from the egyptian God of wisdom, Toth and his Greek counterpart, Hermes. The Hermetica, which is said to be written by Hermes Trismegistus, is generally regarded as the basis of

Western alchemical philosophy and practice. Was this really connected to the legends of the end of time? It was 2012, so the time would fit many of the prophecies. But what did it really mean? I was stunned and mesmerized to find out that there were also more connections.

The Grail comprised 144 facets. And the number 144 was often used as a measurement for many Christian buildings and for some pagan buildings of the first millennium of our era: 144 cells for the church of the Holy Sepulcher at Jerusalem, the mausoleum Saint-Helen in Rome, the Marian church of the Gorizim Mount, the pagan rotunda in Sofia, Italy, at the Church of Saint George, and 144 feet for the Palatine Chapel of Aix-the-Chapel. The origin of this measurement comes from the Revelation (Apocalypse) where John attributes to the periphery of the celestial city 144 cubits (Revelations 21:15 -17).

Have you ever paid attention to any number combination coming your way? If so, did you do any research about it? What did you come to understand?

What do you think this means? Do you think there is a connection between numbers? Have you ever experienced the benefits from wearing crystals? Do you know that many of the reasons why people don't feel the benefits of them are because people are so busy and occupied in their minds that they can't feel the subtle changes coming from the delicate energies from crystals? We have also forgotten how to cultivate this knowledge and as children we might be more sensitive to the gifts from nature; as adults, we tend to forget and exchange the natural vibrations for the more tangible and physical vibrations connected to survival in this third dimension, such as food, money, sex, etc.

Chapter 28

DISCOVERING MAGDALENA

Many sins are forgiven her, because she has loved very much.
—Jesus' words on St. Mary Magdalene

I t seemed to me I was being brought back to where I had started
about 30 years earlier: being a seeker. But this time I had so much
more wisdom within me. As I was so much more grounded and
had been doing a lot of clearing of my emotional body, maybe I could
be a better guide, coach, and healer to others. And so, by the time I
would start working with the crystals, I would be ready for them and
not be drawn into my personal drama, perhaps projecting unresolved
emotions unto others. Now I had come to learn how to identify the
positive from the negative in a whole new way. I was more grounded

and ready to take on more spiritual experiences than I could ever have done before.

I had become an expert in recognizing the "old game" more quickly and identifying resistance within me as well as seeing it within others, and I could more easily let go, not attaching to the old feeling, but instead moving beyond it and hence thinking, choosing, and acting differently. I became an expert in collapsing timelines and breaking through the resistance, not only for myself, but also for my family and my ancestors and maybe even for people with similar stories and backgrounds.

I knew that I wanted to break down the many illusions and much conditioning that I had with me from my childhood and possible previous life times: stuff that was genetically inherited and stuff that I had taken on this lifetime. I know that I'm here to do that. What I mean when I say that is: when we can forgive, forget, heal, let go of, and move on from any negative emotion that prohibits us from living in the light, in joy and harmony, we will no longer need to experience that emotion. And if we can take the chance every time the opportunity arises, we can collapse that timeline, and so move more quickly into higher frequencies where we don't have to experience the hardships again, over and over. We can choose instead to be done with the struggle. And we can from then on live a more happy and free life.

In the winter of 2016, I heard another voice. This time it was from the 13-sided crystal. It was a female voice, and once again I was surprised and uncomprehending.

The crystal told me her name. It was Magdalena, the Swedish version of Magdalene.

I was very surprised and thought about my cousin Magdalena. I couldn't connect the dots at all until much later when I was moving out of our house in the summer of 2017.

The whole thing started earlier, in the summer of 2015, and it all started with a feather. I saw feathers everywhere and birds soaring in the skies.

I thought it had to do with the name of my business, so I changed the name to "Phoenix Light Life Solutions," since I was teaching meditation and giving sessions in transformational energy work from our home. The feather to me also represented having a light heart and that it was a sign that I had worked towards becoming less hard on myself and worked on staying positive. According to old Egyptian legend, usually, the feather was a symbol of Ma'at, the goddess of truth and order. The goddess was always shown wearing an ostrich feather in her hair. The feather by itself was her emblem.

The feather was shown in scenes of the Hall of Ma'at. This hall is where the deceased was judged for his worthiness to enter the afterlife. The seat of the deceased's soul, his heart, was weighed on a balance against the feather of Ma'at. If the heart was free from the impurities of sin, and therefore lighter than the feather, then the dead person could enter the eternal afterlife.

But something inside of me told me that I had to keep searching for something, for what I really should do. I had been drawn to start working with finding my message through looking into my life and what I had learned, with Ted McGrath and *Message to Millions*. His mission was to assist people in finding their own message from their life story, and build a business out from that knowledge. When I was taking part in the Message to Millions program and trying to find out what my message was, I asked the universe/source/ God for the best coach I could get for my process, and I got the best man for the job: Marc Feinberg. He was a coach that worked with the Message to Millions program, and he was the ultimate coach for me at that time. He helped me to see my own greatness and encouraged me to go back to coaching, since he could see that I had a lot of experience with it.

But I wasn't sure I wanted to. Having had a coach very close for a long time, I was fed up and never wanted to have a coach for the rest of my life. And I certainly did not want to be one. But as I started working with Marc, the pure knowing of what I was here to do started to arise from within.

In the fall of 2015, I knew becoming a coach and sharing my story and message was my destiny. I had begun to look for a way to gain more credibility as a coach, so I looked into many certified coaching programs, but nothing appealed to me. At the same time, I was working hard on the dance floor with Pasha, who helped me be the best ballroom dancer I could ever have dreamed of being. Marc helped me set the goals for the year of 2016. Among those goals was winning the US National Championships.

2016 was the beginning of a very challenging time. Robert, my beloved husband, had not played so well for a while and was not bringing in money as he previously had done. This inspired me to become a more accountable partner and to bring in my pieces to the table. My dancing had been very costly, so starting to work was something necessary for me to continue dancing. Luckily a family approached us in Sweden wanting to buy our vacation home, and we saw it as a sign that now was the time to move on. We had not spent a lot of time there lately for many reasons; we were no longer involved with the network as in the old days, and having the kids in an American school made it harder to travel than before. It had become more of a burden than the pleasure it used to be. After the house was sold, and Robert was on tour, the kids and I went to Lapland, Sweden, for our last summer there and packed everything up. It was a beautiful time, full of beautiful midnight sun nights and full of a deep love and gratitude for the time that had been.

I had then also finally found a great coaching program that I was drawn to: the life coach training called the "Quantum Success Coach" program by the Quantum Success Coaching Academy. I started it and loved it, even though it was hard to find time to study, move, and take care of the kids at the same time. Back in the states, Pasha approached me about the dancing competition. We decided to give it a shot even though I had only three weeks to prepare. In September of 2016, we went to Orlando, Florida and competed in the US National championship for Pro-Am dancing. It was an amazing experience. The competition was held at the Disney resorts Swan Hotel. As we arrived at the ground floor, there were ballroom merchants in every corner, selling stunning dresses, amazing shoes, jewelry, and accessories. The night we arrived, we went to peek into the grand ballroom. I was taken aback by the splendor: the huge dance floor, the lights, and the décor. Was this for real? Was I going to dance there the next day? I could hardly believe it. I was so happy just to be there to take part in something so fantastic and to be able to see all the amazing dancers performing. We competed for three days in all styles: standard ballroom: Tango, Waltz, Quickstep, Viennese waltz, and Latin: Cha-cha, Rumba, Jive, and Paso Doble. It was nerve-racking since the competition was much harder than I had experienced before, but realizing that I was going to be dancing in the US nationals, I became more confident in myself and as I entered the dance floor with Pasha, I surrendered to the dream. I was there, and the best thing I could do was to enjoy it. We did great and had so much fun. And to my great surprise and shock we won best amateur Latin Bronze class. I was a National Champion! It then landed a feeling within me that I was becoming a true star: All the inner knowledge that I had learned on my journey in life had taken me to this place in time. I realized that I was a star in every moment: I was a great amateur dancer, a great mom, a great wife, a good friend, and a sweet daughter. Also, I could succeed in any endeavor of my life, from ballroom dancing to moving houses. I found that in truth, I could move mountains. I knew then I had so many powerful tools that I had learned from listening within, and also that I had learned from all the different coaches, people, animals, and situations I had met on my journey. I was indeed a rich woman, and I felt an enormous gratitude and love to all the people that had crossed my road of life and everything that had happened to me. I knew then I had so much to share to the world and the name True Star Coaching was born.

2016 was the year I built up the new coaching business and went to school. It was a big commitment, and we were also looking into simplifying our lives and decreasing financial pressure from a huge house and expensive lifestyle. We decided to sell our 9000 sq.ft. mansion and downsize to make life a bit easier for ourselves.

We bought a smaller house and started renovating. A buyer, who seemed reliable, eventually approached us and since they wanted to move in as soon as school was over, we did everything possible to help them. Unfortunately, or maybe not, Robert was on tour again, and I had to deal with much of the move alone, again! I was desperate and didn't want to go through the last year's dramatic experience, and as I thought the thought of needing help, my friend Frankey contacted me. I had not heard from her in over a year, so I instantly knew it was a sign and asked her if she would be willing to help me get the house ready for the move. She said yes and came and stayed with me for a few days. She helped me sell some furniture and fix garage sales. We had a great time as we shared what had been going on for us during this long time. And interestingly enough, on the day of one of the garage sales, a big turtle came up to the garage front at the back of the house. And stared at us! What did he want, and what did it mean? We didn't think more about it until we started talking about numbers and that I had been seeing the number 33 for a long time. Then I pulled out one of my Vogel crystals, the one with 13 sides. Frankey held the crystal and almost started crying as she connected to the energy of it, and as she did that she looked up the meaning of the numbers 33 and 13 on the computer. She found out that this specific turtle had 13 sides, and it, as well as the number 33, were the numbers of St. Mary Magdalene. Then suddenly it clicked for me: the whole story of the Vogel crystals, how I got them, and why they had gotten the names that they had. They carried the energies and vibrations of the saints. The 13-sided crystal carried the vibration of Saint Mary Magdalene and the 144-sided one, the vibration of Saint George. As tears filled my eyes and shivers went down our spines, we realized the connection and the message from Source/God. What an amazing coincidence this turned out to be—or was it? Maybe this was natural and really what life should be when it's full of miracles and synchronicities? She then looked stunned and said: "Do you know that there is a Sacred Pilgrimage going to the South of France and the Pyrenees to follow the path of Mary Magdalene for Midsummer?" "What?" I gasped. "No, I didn't," I said.

As she pulled up the site on the computer, she said; "It might be too late, and it might be full, but you should definitely take a look." As we looked at the site and read about the trip, I exclaimed, "I have to go there!" and in a couple of minutes I applied to the trip. It turned out they had one space left. I was the 12th person in the group. It was the fifth of June and then the trip was on the 18th. I had no idea what I was throwing myself into. It seemed nuts since I was in the middle of a big move, and the kids were soon going to have their summer break. Since we were renovating the new house, we couldn't move in and had to store all of our stuff, and we didn't have anywhere to live. Robert was going to Europe to play and the kids really wanted to go to Sweden to see their relatives and friends. Our dear friends, Christie and Marcus, offered to let us stay in their little guesthouse until our new house was ready to move into. Problem solved! We sent the kids to Sweden, our three cats to a cat hotel, and our sweet Marta, the poodle, came and stayed with me at Christie and Marcus's house. On the 13th, we signed the closing and moved out. And on the 17th I travelled to Europe.

Chapter 29

THE PURPOSE OF PILGRIMAGE

I am going to my Father's; and though with great difficulty I have got hither, yet now I do not repent me of all the trouble I have been at to arrive where I am. My sword I give to him that shall succeed me in my pilgrimage, and my courage and skill to him that can get it. My marks and scars I carry with me, to be a witness for me that I have fought His battles who will now be my rewarder.
—**John Bunyan**, in *The Pilgrim's Progress* (1678)

I was picked up by John, our course facilitator, at the Toulouse airport, in Languedoc (nowadays L'Occitanie) region, together with two other women from Charlotte. As soon as we landed, the 13 years in Monaco were useful and speaking French again made me feel at home. We drove to a small and picturesque village of Puivert in the lower Pyrenees. We were staying in the most beautiful B&B, called Occitania, after the region L'Occitanie. I had briefly heard about the region, but never completely learned about it. To my great surprise this was the place where the Cathars (meaning, the pure ones) lived. I knew the name because, when I was 20 years old a psychic had told me I had lived as a Cathar in a previous life and most likely I had been killed there. This wasn't something I had thought much about until that moment coming to that region and I didn't know much about them. It was also to this region Mary Magdalene had supposedly come after the resurrection to seek peace and meditation, and she had stayed there for 30 years until her death.

As we arrived at the beautiful and cozy B&B, the hosts and our guides Pete and Anaiya were friendly and loving. They had been arranging trips to this sacred place of the earth for years.

The whole week was a journey, an awakening and initiation process; as well, it was deeply healing. Every morning started with yoga, guided movement, toning, and chakra work followed by breakfast. The facilitators, Marcela and John, were cut out for the job, as they both were deeply immersed into spiritual practices running a spiritual center for mind, body, and soul in Charlotte, as well as very knowledgeable about the region and its story. Later during the day, we would travel and visit sacred places. As we visited and learned about the heritage of the region, its long and rich history, memories started unfolding. And when we visited the famous fortress of Montsegur, at sunrise on Midsummer morning, and I hastily climbed the mountain up to the fortress to arrive in time for the sunrise, memories from the past erupted like an volcano inside of me. As soon as I stepped into the courtyard, I knew I had lost a baby here, a baby who was cut out of my stomach, and as I got up to the top of the fortress wall to witness the daybreak, I had memories of jumping from the edge into the deep gorge of darkness. I had definitely been here before, at least so it felt, or could it have been the energies that I picked up and I was simply misinterpreting them? Whatever it was, it was a huge healing taking place, and as I left the site, I connected with many other visitors who had similar experiences.

At another famous site that we visited, I found myself walking a pathway up the hill. Maybe it was the energy of the earth or the excellent and enchanting guidance by our guides that made me experience what I did. But again, I'm walking as another being from another time, this time as a young virgin lady, dressed in white, carrying a chalice of some kind. I'm barefooted as I'm gently stepping on the pebbles below my feet. When I got up to the top, I knew I was at the right place. I found what looked like a place of sacrifice, with an amazing view of the sky and the valley below. And a flat stone with carvings in it that must have been used many times since it had clear markings. I performed a small ritual of gratefulness and sat there for a while meditating as I was waiting for the others to arrive. Nobody came. Finally, I started walking back down to look for the others, and met one of the guides, who told me I had went off by myself, and the others were at the original site we were going to see. I had totally missed it and passed by, like I had been on a mission.

As a child, I was baptized into Christianity and my first real connection to the bible was when I was confirmed. Even though I enjoyed learning about the bible, there were things in it that never resonated with me. Maybe because they were written in the way they were or maybe how the decades of human interpretation of the sacred text so often forced the religion. Anyhow, I was always interested in finding the truth, the origin, and purpose. The thing I remember the most from that time was when I asked my teacher and priest what a sin was, and he explained it like driving off the road, missing the goal. I liked that parable. So when I learned about the Cathars—their faith and their story as well as the legends about Mary Magdalene—and how they had influenced the region, I wasn't surprised that there was so much more to understand about the origins of Christianity. Who was Mary Magdalene? And why were the Cathars slaughtered and killed by the Christians?

I had always been very taken by the serenity in the old churches and cathedrals in Europe and especially around Christmas and as a student, I researched why churches were built where they were. It was almost always on an old pagan site, where there used to be a temple of some sort. Also there was always the crossing of ley lines in the ground that had been used for the location of the constructions. I have always been wondering why. Why was it important to build on these ley lines and what did they really do? What I later came to learn is that the pagan temples as well as the churches, cathedrals and mosques were built with the sacred geometry rule of the golden proportion and the different venues would turn into sound boxes where each stone would emanate magnetic waves and sounds, that could be interpreted by those sensitive and with insight. Another theory is that the earth itself would have a grid system that would be connected by energetic high spots that would have specific functions.

Visiting the notorious Village of Rennes Le Chateau and The Chapel of St. Mary Magdalene was something that clarified my questions in a way I could never have expected. As I entered the small chapel, and was drawn to the altar in the front, I sat down on the bench, and I looked towards the beautiful indigo painted cupola, covered with tiny stars. In the middle there was a round, stained glass window, and below on the altar, the figure of Magdalene carved into the stone, just like in the Da Vinci Code movie: "She rests at last before starry skies."

As I sat there, I found myself being somehow sucked into a coil or spiral, like a tunnel or vortex of some sort. I immediately fell into deep meditation, and almost felt like I was in trance. I was alone there besides another woman in her 70s, who was also in deep meditation. She seemed to be gone into another space and time. I knew then that this must been a sacred site of some sort, and this was surely what the pagans talked about: a portal, the connection to other dimensions. And maybe that was what the mystery was about all of the time? I had not been there before and I didn't know anything about the amazing and fascinating story about the chapel and what had been going on there, but some of it was told in the movie The Da Vinci Code and also in a book I had had in my bookshelf for years, *Holy Blood, Holy Grail*, but never read. It was the first time I ever have had a conscious experience of a portal or vortex.

As the days continued, and we worked on clearing and balancing our chakras in the morning, the holy sites we visited emphasized the experience. When the day came to crawl into the initiation caves at Ornolac, our guide, Anaiya, told us about their purpose and meaning; "The Cathar Initiation Caves at Ornolac in the Ariege region of Southern France continue to beckon the spiritual travellers to their initiatory door. This three-part cave complex houses the Eglise (Church), the Hermit, and the Bethlehem Cave. These underground retreats, places of meeting with the 'Almighty Creative Essence,' offered the Cathars a safe and peaceful dwelling place. We are told that in these caves the initiate would begin to access the state of the living Soul, the state of the 'Pure One' or 'Perfect One' (parfait). When the timing was right, the disciple would go through the 'Mystical Door,' and come back into the world to devote themselves to suffering mankind, in service to Christ.

"The Eglise is the first stage of the Initiation. It is where the perfect one would say goodbye to the material world and enter the Eglise for a period of three years. The Eglise is very much about the letting go of materialism, material traps, and addictions, external responsibilities, ties and contracts, all kinds of greed, wealth, financial power, and status. It marks the beginning of a serious spiritual change, a step and stage along the way upon which there is no return. Here is the moment where you renounce the god of the material world and all his empty promises and enter the dwelling place of the Living Soul."

We started climbing up the steep mountain and entered into the cave system of seven "rooms," each representing a chakra. I so wanted to go all the way but felt it important to listen within myself. And only felt like going to the fourth. After crawling on my stomach and shuffling myself forward through all of the narrow tunnels and entering the magnificent chambers, we came into the fourth one, the heart chakra; it was a higher chamber so we could easily stand up in it; it was very peaceful but at the same time very thrilling.

I knew I had to face my fears, so I decided to crawl back to the third chamber, the solar plexus chakra, where the power resided. I was afraid since I didn't know what kind of creatures I would meet there and there were also several tunnels in the system so I could easily have taken the wrong one, not knowing the way back. I finally came back to the chamber and I sat there alone against the mountain wall. I only had a small light coming from my cell phone since my head light was flickering and didn't stay lit. I knew I had to turn it off to be able to experience what I needed to, so I did. It was pitch black but even though I could see all kinds of shadows and symbols in there, maybe it was in my inner vision and it scared me a little. I focused on unconditional love and started to tone, to sing a melody... the negative feeling started to disappear. Was it within me everything was happening or was it the energies inside the mountain or from the people that had been initiated there over the centuries?

The last day had arrived and we worked on the seventh chakra, the connection to the all, the one, source/ God. It was about integration. The whole week had built up to this crescendo. And in the morning, we were guided to heal the union between the sacred masculine and feminine energy, that both reside within us. I fell into big tears as finally my inner man was seen and heard. He was so tired of working so hard, running the show, being accountable, taking care of the house, the kids, and everybody. He was honorable and accountable but extremely worn out and tired. So arose the sacred feminine aspect of me, and as I sat there in the sacred circle watching and observing, my hands formed a union, representing the union within me. My feminine aspect took over, and said to the masculine aspect of me, "Don't worry, you have worked so hard. Let me take over now, so that you can rest." It was profound. No wonder I had been feeling what I had been feeling all these years. My longing for the perfect man meant that every man that I had ever met in my life had to suffer feeling never enough for me—because deep inside of me, my inner man was never enough for me. It was time for the big healing, to be a whole human being, integrated within. The union between the masculine and the feminine had taken place and I was now whole in a way I had never been before.

Have you ever gone on a pilgrimage? If so, where did you go and why? What was your experience? What do you think about the origin of Christianity and all other religions? What is your belief? Have you experienced your sacred feminine self or masculine self? Do you feel integrated and whole?

Chapter 30

THE UNION

"But let there be spaces in your togetherness and let the winds of the heavens dance between you. Love one another but make not a bond of love: let it rather be a moving sea between the shores of your souls."

—Khalil Gibran

As soon as the Pilgrimage ended, I called Robert who I had not talked to for the whole week, since I wanted to give my fullest attention to the spiritual growth for the most amount of benefit. We spoke over Facetime. He looked at me saying; "You are radiant, and so beautiful. That woman I want to be married to."

It was Sunday and life had so perfectly orchestrated the timing; Robert's next tournament was the French Open, in Paris, the week after. And I was going there to see him, since he was going to be gone for several weeks on tour for the rest of the summer. We were going to be alone for the first time in months. I was so looking forward to going there but I was also a bit nervous; I didn't know what to expect. I felt open like a treasure chest; full, contained, rich, and whole. But also open, vulnerable, sensitive, like a newborn child and a bit fragile—and afraid to be abused. How would I be received in the world and how would Robert receive me and treat me when he would see the new, integrated me? But there was a new sense of trust within me. Almost a feeling like it didn't matter what would happen. What will be will be. This was new. I never felt so secure in my own skin before. Yes, I had experienced knowing that I could deal with things and I had been strong. But this time it was different, I wasn't alone anymore, I had the sacred union, with the man and woman within me. It was no longer necessary to search for *him*, the perfect man, since I had him within me and I knew that was all that I needed to know. And knowing how The Law of Attraction works, I knew that I would attract the real human man that was perfect for me, whether it was Robert or not. I had faith.

I met Robert, and I felt strong but at the same time fragile. Would I have the strength I needed to keep myself balanced? Would I default to choose to go back to old patterns or choose to remember and be strong enough to live out from my new-found core? My big challenge would be if Robert didn't play well and maybe started to project his own disappointment on me.

As I had united the dualities within myself, I came to understand that everybody I met on my life's journey was showing me something about myself. They were all representing different aspects of me, like the archetypes in the tarot deck. The people I had met on the road were merely reflections of myself; the coach's sides that I didn't like were the sides I didn't like about myself; the parts that I liked and admired were the sides that I lacked and wanted to have more of. The people I admired had what I wanted to have that I didn't think I had myself. On my long journey, it was finally established in my mind, body, and soul, that there is no one to blame for anything. I'd chosen and created my experiences all along even if I had not been conscious about it, I had created all the experiences to become the one I was. Maybe I had already decided, as a higher consciousness in another dimension before coming to this earth what my journey was going to be or maybe they were happening as a result of my previous choices and feelings. I am today incredibly grateful for everything that I have experienced and rather than running and fighting from the resistance and pain, I have learned to embrace it, being grateful for the understanding that when a difficult situation or challenge arises, I have the possibility to choose not to be sucked into the old story but to understand that I can change the situation by focusing on the lesson that can be learned, and what I don't want to bring into my reality. And when I know what I don't want to bring in, I can focus on what I truly desire and can allow that into my experience and life.

So when I finally flew to Paris, I was a new woman, whole and alive. When I arrived in Orly, I took a motorcycle taxi, something I had never done before, and as we were zigzagging through the heavy traffic with what felt like the speed of light, I saw the symbolism of my life; I had succeeded in driving on the path and learned how to steer through the obstacles to get to my destination. And as I finally embraced my beloved Robert, I knew that the whole time the goal of my life—my destination—had been love, to find true love, and that I had found it within myself. I realized that the truth was I had never been in my husband's shadow, I had just hidden my true starlight, the true love, my whole and authentic self, from myself, and by doing so from the world.

When Robert entered the room and saw me, he was in awe. He was taken by my energy and was so attracted to me. He lit up like the sun, just like a kid on Christmas Eve. His eyes lit up as he saw me, his wife, as a new woman. Our union was beautiful, like newlyweds, passionate, tender, like new lovers discovering each other for the first time. It was a sacred meeting. We were one unity. And I truly love my husband, my twin flame.

Chapter 31

THE ENDING

"You must be the change you wish to see in the world"
—Mahatma Gandhi

As I'm sitting on the hotel bed, I'm flicking through Facebook and see one of my friends liking this company, called The Author Incubator. I think it was the Feather that I saw on the logo, which in my subconscious mind gave it away, as well as hearing Angela Lauria, the founder's voice. It was familiar; it was like a calling, for me to take a new step, to take on a new mission. I felt resonance with her message, like something old within me recognizing the truth, and whispering into my soul that now was the time; I was going to write a book! I didn't know how it was going to happen, since I was still going to school getting certified as a coach and being in charge of the renovation of our new house. But I thought it might work since I was staying with friends; I have time. And it was time to once again step up to the plate and be a True Star.

This is what I wrote:

The year is 2017. I'm sitting in my hotel room 3301 in Trianon Palace, Versailles, Paris, France. The balcony doors are open and the fresh country air from the park close to the Chateau de Versailles is caressing my skin as I am writing this.

As I started writing my book and looking back at my journey I came to understand that the term "seeker" is tricky since if I am constantly identifying myself as a seeker that is what I believe I am and will manifest hence never becoming a finder. Telling myself I am a finder seems more reasonable. I want to find the truth and my true full potential.

I realized that all the knowledge that I had accumulated on my journey needed to be shared and if now was not the time when would it be? I knew I had to jump on the train; I didn't have a moment to lose. And as I had healed the sacred masculine and feminine within me, I no longer needed Robert as I had done before. Now I was strong enough to be independent, stand on my own two feet and live on my own, but I wanted to be with him, I wanted to discover more of myself, him and what it meant to be in a sacred union together so even though we had struggled for so long in our relationship I knew that it would be the best thing forward. So I decided to push through even though it looked impossible.

So to end this book I'd like to share some of the things I have found so far:

- That to be a True Star is to act out of my truth and my full potential. It is when I am fully aligned with my higher self. From this alignment with my inner sun, my inner star, I can create miracles, manifest and discover that I am a multidimensional being.

- That my truth and my true potential is something I am discovering day by day, and as I am peeling the "onion" letting go, shedding everything that I no longer am, I am becoming more and more of myself also realizing that I am just a piece of consciousness, a part of the bigger picture, the whole, source, the one, call it what you want.

- That we always have a choice how to react in any situation and can either choose to be a victim of circumstances or chose to grow, learn and expand.

- If something doesn't feel good it's either a sign that we are not aligned with our true and higher self and need to make a change within our self, or it's a sign that we are compromising our own truth.

- That feelings and emotions are not good or bad, they are only vibrations, energy, letting us know where we are on the emotional scale. We can choose to move up or down the guidance system we call the emotional scale since we have free will, and if we like to feel better, we only need to take a step at the time, raising our own vibration, our own frequency.

- That we are all creators and cannot blame anything or anybody for what we are feeling or experiencing since we are co-creating everything in our lives. We create by manifesting our thoughts, with our feelings, our vibration.

- New levels of myself,—the journey will never stop, it's constantly evolving, and it's an infinite quest into the mystery called life.

There are many dimensions to this existence. The one we are currently living in is very dense. We are multidimensional beings having a physical experience and can excel to higher dimensions by making better choices, aligning ourselves with our higher self.

- That I can find peace within by embracing the uncomfortable and negative emotions and seeing the gifts in them. And if a certain emotion or experience is coming back over and over it is still more to see and understand until I can fully heal and to let go.
- That the Law of Attraction is a universal law stating that like attracts like. What I feel/vibrate within is what I will attract or create on the outside. It is what I feel that makes the difference not what I say.
- By giving something attention I am feeding it, no matter if it is positive or negative. Wherever I put my attention, grows.
- I found that I could raise my own frequency by letting go of the pain, the blame, the misery and by breathing in the truth; being honest with myself and honoring what I feel, by saying yes to the moment connecting to the eternal source within.
- That by nourishing the truth; that I am love, light, and joy I would create more harmony within me and around me.

I have to ask myself how much does it cost me not to be aligned with my higher self? My experience is that by continuing to live in oblivion and denial, I compromise my higher self. Over time it might cause imbalances in my own life such as depression, sickness, misery, separation and loss. The price we pay for living in that illusion is that we suffer. How wonderful would life be if we all came to understand that we are but one energy, like the vast ocean, we are solely unique drops of that infinite water? As we realize who we are we can feel whole again.

When you have started to know who you are and what feels good stick with what feels good in your stomach. Trust your inner guidance system. If something doesn't feel right, speak up; don't go against your inner knowing. You know what is best for you. Even though the person who tells you what to do might see where you are stuck don't allow that person to push you towards what seems right to them. They don't have the same frequencies as you. They can't know because they are not you. They didn't come down to this planet when you did and they don't know the journey you are on. You might not yet be ready. You will know when you are ready for your next step. Nobody else will know it for you. You are the one who can set yourself free. The truth is nobody can do it for you. We can seek advice and guidance from others and it's important to do that at times but don't allow their voice to be louder than the voice from your inner higher self.

I have sought advice many times in my life and I suggest that you do that too, if you want to speed up the process of becoming more of yourself and living a more free and authentic life. But remember you are the one choosing and creating your life and its experiences. To change the world and make it a better place, we have to start with ourselves, filling our own cup, loving and accepting ourselves and from that space we can start to overflow, to share with others and give authentically. You came here for a reason, remember who you are, and know that you have what it takes. You are indeed a True Star, and you can allow your True Starlight to shine from within and let that higher self of yours, your True Star guide you. Be Stellar and be the True Star in your movie!

What are the things you have come to understand reading this book? Do you resonate with some of it or does it seem very weird and awkward? What do you know is true? How can you become more aligned with your True Self, your higher self? How can you become a True Star living in your fullest potential?

ACKNOWLEDGMENTS

A thank you simply doesn't feel enough when it comes to expressing how grateful and happy I am to everyone who has crossed my life path since without his or her interaction my life wouldn't be what it has become. But here I go, THANK YOU! I know that somewhere somehow we decided to interact with each other before we entered into this reality. Thanks also to all of you who inspired me with your wisdom and knowledge; without your help I would not have come to know what I know today.

And thanks to those that supported me emotionally, mentally, and spiritually standing by me and supporting me in this world and beyond to get the book out into the world.

You are all amazing, and indeed you are True Stars.

The list is long, and if I missed anyone, please know that you are equally as important as everybody else. Thanks to my mom, dad who decided to support me to share my story even though it would disclose the family secrets. They both agreed that sharing our past could help others to grow. Thanks to my brother Eric who encouraged me to be authentic and thanks to my beloved husband Robert for his inspiration, strength and support. For being my mirror, giving me the chance to heal from the past and uniting the aspects of myself.

Thanks to our beautiful children Thea and Ceasar for being patient with me and taking so much more responsibility, making it possible for me to work and write. Thanks to Marta, our poodle, my constant loving companion and Simba, Grace and Sophie our three cats for all their loving purring and support.

To the Morgan James Publishing team: Special thanks to David Hancock, CEO & Founder for believing in me and my message. To my Author Relations Manager, Margo Toulouse, thanks for making the process seamless and easy. Many more thanks to everyone else, but especially Jim Howard, Bethany Marshall, and Nickcole Watkins.

Thanks to Peter Ljungberg, Jonas Philipson and the Ideal Village for bringing meditation and consciousness to the world. Thanks to The Body Shop Sweden and all of my friends in Sweden who worked there. Thanks to Sandy Levy Lundin and her family and friends. Thanks to Roger Nilson and Premleena Wettergran who without them I would never have met Robert. Thanks to everybody at Mullingstorp, Victoria Eriksson and Bengt Stern for all their amazing work. Thanks to OSHO and Osho Risk. Thanks to all friends and inhabitants of the Village in Lapland. Thanks to Maria and Lars for being great friends and Godparents to Ceasar. Thanks to Ballroom 5 and all the great dancers, instructors and students I have met in the Ballroom world, especially Pasha, Karolina and Daniel. Thanks to Christy and Evelyn and The Quantum Coaching Academy. And my coaching buddies; Hardy, Debra and Poppy. Thanks to Anne Glasgow, Marc Feinberg, Joe Eigo, Frankey Craig, Suzanne Lie. Thanks to my friends for all of your help during the writing process: Heidi Triezeberg Morgan, Shannon

Maxwell, Sherry George, Carolyn Bell, Catherine Lavallee, Katherine Currier, Helena Raines, Joshua Wilson,, Annika Tedewall, Christine Conte, Thank you to John and Marcela McBride for initiating the trip to France, and to Anaiya Sophia and Pete for the work you do and for inspiring me to write. Thanks to the Burch Family for their loving and supporting friendship. Thanks to Robert Whitlock for helping out with the cover photo and Glenn Roberson for the author photo. And thanks to everybody at the Author Incubator who so lovingly supported me to make this happen, especially Rae, Maggie, Angela and Cynthia. And a big thank you to Sharon Mitchell who helped out in the last minute. Thanks to my cousin Jinjee for last minute editing. And finally, a big thanks to all my clients who I love so much and have made me a better person and coach.

About the Author

Ebba P Karlsson, is the Swedish International True Star coach and founder of True Star Coaching. She is a certified Law of Attraction and Creating money Coach and member of ICF, with 20 years of experience in meditation, personal self- development and leadership. Married to Professional Golfer Robert Karlsson, she coaches high-performers and their partners, to live a more fulfilling life.

THANK YOU

Dearest fellow traveler,

Thank you for reading my book. It means so much to me to be able to share my story with you. It is my deepest intention that it has given you something to think about and sparked something within you that can lead you forward on your quest. Maybe you will find what is necessary for you to take the next step in your life?

I would so like to know what you thought about the book, if you enjoyed reading it and if the questions got you thinking. Please share any thoughts or questions you might have by sending me an email to me at ebba@truestarcoaching.com

If you are interested in going deeper on your journey or getting some assistance in finding your True Starlight head over to my website: www.truestarcoaching.com and take the quiz.

Be Stellar!

Ebba

Morgan James
Speakers Group

www.TheMorganJamesSpeakersGroup.com

We connect Morgan James published authors with live and online events and audiences who will benefit from their expertise.